THUNDERSTORM
in CHURCH

Thunderstorm in Church

by
Louise A. Vernon

GREENLEAF PRESS
Lebanon, Tennessee

I extend appreciative thanks to Professor Muriel B. Ingham, of California State University, San Diego, who acted as interpreter on our visit to Wittenberg, Eisenach, Wartburg Castle, and Eisleben, enabling me to use many details about Martin Luther's life that would not have been available otherwise.

I am grateful to her and to Helen Farr, teacher of German at California State University, San Diego, for translating Ernst Kroker's book, *Katharina von Bora*, specifically for my use.

CONTENTS

MARTIN LUTHER AT HOME

THIRTY men, women, and children waited in the large dining hall of the Black Cloister in Wittenberg, Germany, for the ten o'clock breakfast, the first of two daily meals. University students, houseguests, cousins, and the Luther children with their beloved Aunt Lena had watched Frau Luther and the hired help put platters of food on the table. Everyone was hungry.

"Where is Dr. Luther?" a student asked in a plaintive voice.

"In his tower room," someone answered.

"Frau Luther, has your husband forgotten to eat?" another groaned.

Laughter rippled through the group.

Frau Luther laughed, too, then sighed. "I'll send one of the children after him. Hans, you go this time."

At the stairway, Hans felt a pat on his shoulder. A visiting preacher beamed at him.

9

"If you grow up to be as famous as your father, someone will have to remind you to eat," the preacher said.

Hans flinched. Intended as a joke, the words hurt a secret, precious place inside himself — his sense of self-worth. It was bad enough to be teased by his older cousins living at the Black Cloister, but to have outsiders begin to kid him about his father really hurt.

As he climbed the steep, winding stairway to the fourth floor, Hans felt himself growing smaller and smaller somewhere inside. How could anyone be as famous as Martin Luther, his father? Father was the man who said that only God forgave sins, not the church. He had been called a heretic, threatened with death, and excommunicated. But Father kept on preaching and writing that the church had no right to take people's money in exchange for telling them their sins were forgiven.

Because of Father, thousands of people in Germany and other countries worshiped God with joy instead of fear. Hundreds wrote to Father and thanked him for helping them understand God's Word. Dozens came to the Black Cloister to discuss how to run the new church that had sprung up from Father's writings and preaching.

"Everybody asks me for advice," Father sometimes complained, "but I don't know whether they really want to learn from me or if they are spying on me."

The visitors called the new church *Lutheran*.

"Don't use my name for the church. I'm a bad Lutheran." Father laughed. "What is Luther? What have I done, poor stinking sack of worms that I am, that Christ's children should be called by my unholy name? The teaching is not mine. Let's call ourselves Christians, after Jesus whose teachings we follow."

But his protests were useless. People kept on calling the new church by Father's name. The membership grew larger every day, and many of the men who felt called to preach the Word visited the Black Cloister to talk to Martin Luther.

Father is a famous man, Hans thought, *and I'm just a nobody.* Of course, he was only a boy, but that thought did not help. People expected him to be someone special. But what was he supposed to be?

Filled with these thoughts, Hans stood outside the closed door of his father's study, afraid to knock. Was Father reading, writing, praying — or was he sick again with one of his headaches, stomachaches, or dizzy spells?

Hans heard someone coming up the stairs. Lenchen, his younger sister, appeared twirling a fresh rose. Behind her, Tölpel, Father's beloved dog, scampered across the bare, wooden floor, his toenails making sharp clicks at each step. Tölpel nosed his way between Hans and Lenchen, sat down, and thumped his tail expectantly.

"Did Father answer?" Lenchen asked.

"I haven't knocked yet."

"Well, hurry up. It's almost ten o'clock, and everybody is waiting."

Everybody included Mother, Aunt Lena, the three smaller Luther children — Martin, Paul, and baby Margarete, together with the eleven older cousins living with the Luther family, the university students boarding at the Black Cloister, the hired

11

help, and the usual houseguests, who changed from time to time.

"I don't think Father wants to be disturbed." Hans was not ready yet to confide in his sister about his feeling of worthlessness. "Maybe he wants to fast today, like the time he locked that door and didn't have anything to eat or drink for three days."

Lenchen stopped twirling her rose. Her eyes widened. "What did Mother do?"

Hans laughed, remembering. "She hired a workman to remove the door."

"And then what?"

"All Father said was, 'What harm am I doing?' So maybe we'd better not disturb him."

"We have to," Lenchen exclaimed. "We can't eat until he leads us in our prayers."

"Maybe he has one of his headaches —" Hans began, but a glance from Lenchen stopped him. He made a fist ready to pound the thick oak door. Then he dropped his arm. "I — I can't," he said in a hoarse whisper.

"Why, Hans Luther, I do believe you're *afraid*." Lenchen's eyes widened again, this time with scorn. "Who could be afraid of Father?"

Lots of people, Hans wanted to say. Kings and princes and even the pope in Rome. Bishops and priests. Medical doctors. Church doctors, like Father himself. Lawyers. City councils. Yes, lots of people were afraid of Father. *Including me,* Hans admitted to himself.

His two brothers, Martin, Jr., and Paul, were too little to know the strange fear of being sons of a famous father. And of course baby Margarete didn't have to worry about such problems, nor Lenchen, either. Girls had nothing to worry about, anyway. All they had to do was learn how to keep house. They didn't have to worry about making a name for themselves.

But it was strange to be afraid of Father. *Then why am I afraid?* Hans asked himself. Didn't Father laugh, sing, and play with his children every night before they went to bed? Didn't he joke and make up little poems to amuse them? Didn't he tell exciting stories from Aesop about cunning foxes and mean wolves? Yes, but Father was also the most famous man in Europe. *Does everyone expect me to become famous too?* Hans wondered. It was a question he knew he'd be living with for a long time.

Still, he wouldn't want to be a girl. His teenage girl cousins giggled all the time and chattered a lot about getting married. Boys had more adventures. Hans and his friends, Lippus Melanchthon and Jost Jonas, sons of Father's good friends, could explore the town wall, go to the market square, walk along the Elbe River, play in the barn, or examine the fruit trees in Mother's orchard.

Lenchen shook his arm. "Hans, quit daydreaming. Go tell Mother and Aunt Lena we're coming. I'll call Father myself." Over her shoulder she hissed, "Coward," and tickled Tölpel's nose with the rose.

The word *coward* seared Hans like the hot, three-legged iron kettle base in the kitchen fireplace he'd once touched on a dare from one of his older cousins. But he pretended he hadn't heard Lenchen and lingered at the door.

Lenchen knocked.

13

Hans heard Father's muffled voice. "Come in."
Hans regained his courage. He reached for the handle and opened the door.

"Father, it's time to eat," he announced.

Standing in the doorway, Hans suddenly saw Father as others saw him: the broad shoulders, the plump face with a deep dimple in the chin, the brown hair and deep-set, piercing brown eyes. Behind Father the table, windowsill, chair, and stool were covered as usual with lecture notes, letters, books, petitions, and galley proofs. Every day that Father wasn't sick or on a journey, he answered letters, prepared lectures and sermons, or checked galleys.

"Time to eat?" Father echoed. "What a bother. I have so much work to do I don't feel like eating. Tell the Morning Star of Wittenberg to go ahead without me."

Father had many pet names for Mother. Sometimes he called her *Herr Kathe,* as if she were a man. Sometimes he called her his rib, and then he and Mother would laugh.

"But Father, we're your *family,*" Lenchen reminded him, crowding in ahead of Hans. She held out the rose. "I picked it for you just this morning."

Father was delighted. He loved flowers. "A glorious work of art by God Himself," he exclaimed. "If a man had the capacity to make just one rose he would be given an empire. But," he added as if to himself, "the countless gifts of God are esteemed as nothing because they're always present."

"We're present, too, Father."

Tölpel wriggled past Lenchen and jumped up on

14

Hans suddenly saw Father as others saw him.

Father. He laughed, patted Tölpel's head, and reached for his coat.

Hans darted ahead of Lenchen down the long hall, but she caught up with him. "Now, see?" she challenged. "What was there to be afraid of?"

Hans winced. How could he explain? Thousands of people weren't afraid of Martin Luther. He had shown them the joyous message of Scripture. He had brought the Bible to the German people in their own language. He always said what he believed without fear.

"You'd better not let Father know you're afraid," Lenchen murmured.

Hans clenched his fists. "All right, so I am afraid. Quit talking about it."

Lenchen's face softened. "Oh, that's different. You've confessed, the way Father says people have to do. I won't tease you anymore, and I won't tell Father."

"Why can't we live like other people?" Hans burst out. "Maybe things would be different." There wouldn't be so many people asking questions that made him feel small. "If we could only eat together, just our own family and nobody else."

"That's selfish."

"No, it's not. Families come first."

"Not with Father. He says charity comes first," Lenchen said.

"Well, I don't think it's right for people to come here and eat and not even offer to pay for a meal. You know how Mother tries to make ends meet."

"Father says if you give freely, God gives freely in return."

16

"I suppose that's why Mother always feeds the beggars who come to our door," Hans reflected, "but I heard Father say some beggars are more proud inside than some rich men he knows."

"Well, just so our dog Tölpel doesn't become proud." Lenchen laughed. "He certainly knows how to beg for his food."

At breakfast everyone ate with hearty appetites. Tölpel sat near Father with open mouth and motionless eyes. Father laughed and called everyone's attention to the dog. "Oh, if I could only pray the way this dog watches for a scrap of food. All his thoughts are centered on the next bite." He dropped a bit of food into Tölpel's mouth. "The dog is a faithful animal. No wonder they are held in high esteem."

In good humor, Father changed the subject. "Did you ever notice that girls begin to talk and to stand on their feet sooner than boys?"

Hans winced. It seemed as if every remark lately jabbed at his self-worth. His girl cousins giggled across the table at him.

"But weeds always grow more quickly than good crops," Father teased.

Hans felt a twinge of triumph.

"I don't worry about the boys," Father went on, "because a boy supports himself, no matter what country he's in, as long as he's willing to work." Father nodded toward Hans' boy cousins and then toward the girl cousins. "But the poor girls — that's a different story. They must have a staff to lean on." With mock seriousness he recited a little poem from memory:

17

"A red apple may look good and inviting,
And yet worminess hide.
So a girl with the worst disposition
May be pretty outside."

The girls giggled.

"Oh, Father, stop teasing us," Lenchen exclaimed.

The meal continued with much laughter and talking. After breakfast Father took tiny Margarete in his arms and nuzzled her until she crowed with delight. When she needed her diaper changed, Mother took her out.

"Our Lord God has to put up with many a murmur and stink from us," Father mused, "worse than a mother must endure from her child. But just as a mother's love is stronger than the filth on a child, so the love of God toward us is stronger than the dirt of sin that clings to us."

While Mother was in another room with Margarete, a visitor at the Black Cloister looked slyly at Father. "Dr. Luther," he said, "I have heard that you rely on your wife more than on Christ."

At first Father frowned, then he burst into laughter. "In family affairs, I defer to Kathe. Otherwise, I am led by the Holy Spirit." He added with a chuckle, "If I should ever marry again, I would hew myself an obedient wife out of stone; otherwise, in desperation I obey all women."

The students still lingered at the table, as always encouraging Father to talk. One of them asked what the Luther boys would do when they grew up. Hans ducked down. Why was so much being said about growing up?

18

"I intend to send my children away when they're grown," Father replied. "Any of them who wants to be a soldier, I'll send to Hans Loeser. Dr. Jonas and Philip will have any of them who want to study, and if one wants to work with his hands, I'll turn him over to a peasant."

"What about the law as a profession?" another student asked.

"Law?" Father spat out the word. "If I had a hundred sons I wouldn't let one of them become a lawyer. No lawyer honors God. They're only interested in themselves."

Father was working himself into one of his rages. He glared at Hans, Martin, and Paul. "If any of you became a lawyer, I'd hang you on the gallows," he thundered.

Mother tried to soothe him. "Now, Doctor," she began.

"A good strong burst of anger refreshes the system," Father interrupted.

"Do be careful," Mother went on. "You may bring on one of your headaches, and then we'll have to send for a doctor."

Father didn't like medical doctors any more than he liked lawyers.

"Aren't you a doctor?" little Martin asked.

"Yes."

"Can't you put bandages on yourself where you hurt?"

"I'm a church doctor," Father explained. "A medical doctor heals the body and a church doctor heals the spirit." He smiled at little Martin. "You must be a preacher when you grow up and baptize, preach,

19

administer the sacrament, visit the sick, and comfort the sorrowful."

Calm once again, Father prayed with the household before going to his study. "Dear heavenly Father, You have given me the honor of being a father. Now grant me Your mercy and bless me that I rule and nourish my dear wife, children, and household in a godly and Christian manner. Give me the wisdom and strength to bring them up well. Give them also the heart and desire to follow Your teaching and to be obedient. Amen."

After Father left the room, the visiting preacher who had talked to Hans before took him aside. "Does your father get upset very often?"

Hans thought a moment, then nodded. Father frequently *did* get upset.

"Strange," the visiting preacher murmured. "Why would God use a man with such a quick temper?"

"But he laughs a lot, too," Hans said in defense of Father. His own problem of being a nobody dissolved in a strong feeling of family loyalty. Besides, Father prayed every day for guidance.

"Father knows he has a temper and he prays about it. God guides him. He guides us all."

And Hans knew that was true.

TROUBLE AT THE MARKET SQUARE

IN THE afternoon Mother decided to show Lenchen how to market. Little Martin clamored to go along.

"Hans, you come, too," Mother said.

Hans was glad to leave his Latin lesson and Jerome Weller, his quiet, moody tutor. He followed Mother, Lenchen, and little Martin out the door. As they walked along Hans began to feel uneasy. It wasn't just the overcast sky. An unpleasant incident had happened the last time he and his two friends, Lippus and Jost, had visited the market square.

Three peasant boys had thrown rotten cabbage heads at Hans and his friends. Not only that, the peasant boys threatened to toss all three town boys into the stinking, open ditch that ran the length of the street. The ditch carried garbage and raw sewage. How awful to be pushed into it. Hans shuddered, remembering. How Aunt Lena would scold! And with reason. It would take many washings

21

to remove the stench of rotting garbage — and worse — from their clothes.

As if in answer to his thoughts, Hans spied the same three boys, about his own age, standing behind a cheese stall. When they saw him, they stuck their tongues out at him. Thank goodness Mother hadn't noticed. She was busy teaching Lenchen how to shop. Little Martin tugged at his mother's skirt. Mother bent down and gently pushed Martin toward Hans. "Please take care of your brother. I'm too busy with Lenchen to watch him."

Hans sensed trouble coming. What if a fight developed with the peasant boys? Still, they probably wouldn't throw him in the ditch with Martin there. Grown-ups could always be counted on to come to the aid of small children.

"Stay right here," Hans whispered to his brother. But Martin, bouncing in excitement at his first trip to market, swung out of Hans' grasp and darted toward a stall where live geese waddled and honked.

"Let's buy a goose," Martin called. "Father likes them."

Whenever Father saw the geese in the courtyard of the Black Cloister, he was sure to say something about swans. He had a stone swan in his study. "If you burn a goose, from its ashes rises a swan," Father would tell visitors. They would explain to each other, "Oh, he means something greater arises from ashes. He's referring to the great Bohemian martyr, John Huss, who was burned at the stake for his religious beliefs. *Hus* means goose, you know."

Little Martin squatted down and talked to the geese. Hans eyed the three peasant boys wriggling through the crowd and coming closer. He and his friends had avoided a fight the last time, but Hans expected a showdown someday soon. Not today, he hoped. Not without Lippus and Jost. Hans was sure the three of them together could lick their weight in peasants.

Hans did not dare turn his back or edge away, and he certainly would not dare get into a fight. Not with Mother here. If Aunt Lena had come, it would be different. She knew how to overlook certain things boys felt they had to do.

Such thoughts were of no help now. Hans saw the peasant boys slip with seeming innocence past townspeople bargaining at the various stalls.

There was one hope. The overcast sky promised one of the frequent sudden showers Wittenberg was accustomed to. When thunder and lightning came with these quick storms, peasants believed the devil was loose, and they would hide until the storm let up.

An ear-piercing shriek rose above the chatter of buyers and sellers. A peasant woman with arms upraised ran up to Mother and shook her fist in Mother's face.

"I know who you are, Katharina von Bora, you sinful, fallen woman. Go home to your den of iniquity. You don't belong with decent people."

Mother moved away, but the peasant blocked her path. Townspeople, gasping and muttering among themselves, formed a semicircle around the two women. Shocked, Hans watched. What would Father say when he learned about this incident?

"Aristocrat or not, you had no right to marry,"

23

the peasant woman stormed. "You broke your vows. You are Christ's bride, not man's."

Mother, whose tongue was usually as nimble as her fingers, clasped one hand over the other and in total silence let the woman rage on. At last the peasant woman allowed her friends to lead her away, still shouting and waving her fists.

The townspeople backed off in little groups, talking and nodding toward the Luthers.

Little Martin looked up at Hans. "Why are people pointing to us?"

"Because they know we're Martin Luther's family."

"Don't they like us?"

"Not everyone."

"Why not?"

"Because of what Father did about the church. Stop asking questions and come on." He guided Martin out of earshot of the gossiping people. He wished the summer storm would hurry up and soak everybody. To these people Father had been like a storm. A thunderstorm in church.

The people at the stalls went back to work, calling out their wares in singsong voices. Behind Hans, two women started talking. The three peasant boys had disappeared. "So that's Frau Luther," a woman exclaimed. "I do believe she's buying cheese."

"You seem surprised," the other woman laughed.

"Is she too lazy to make her own cheese? She has cows enough at the Black Cloister, I understand."

"Oh, she's not lazy. No one can ever accuse her of that, I must say in all fairness. So many people live at the Black Cloister she has a time feeding them all."

"Surely the five Luther children don't eat that much," the other woman sniffed.

"Five children! There are sixteen."

"But that isn't possible."

"Well, eleven of them are relatives. Most of them are Dr. Luther's nephews and nieces. Then, of course, students and visitors stay there, too."

A third woman joined the other two. "You're talking about Frau Luther, aren't you? They say she runs a house, a hotel, and a hospital there at the Black Cloister."

A man leaning on a cane had been listening. He, too, had something to say. "An odd assortment of young people, students, young girls, widows, old women, and children live in the doctor's home. Things never really settle down there, and many pity Luther because of it."

Another man spoke up. "Yes, you do well to pity Dr. Luther. Imagine being a bachelor for forty-two years and then marrying! Now he has all those people to feed. He's ill so much himself he should have been a medical doctor instead of a church doctor."

"You have to admit he has courage, though," a woman said. "He didn't leave Wittenberg during the plague nine years ago — said his Bible protected him."

"That may be," the man with the cane retorted, "but I hear that some of his followers want to become Catholics again. Dr. Luther won't even let them buy their relatives out of purgatory. He and his Reformation. To think that he's living in that monastery and he's not even a Catholic."

"But Elector John Frederick gave it to him, you know, and the city lets him have his water free."

"He's no better than a thief, if you ask me," the man snapped.

"Be careful what you say. There are people here in Wittenberg who will fight if you say one word against Dr. Luther."

Someone called Mother's name. Hans clenched his fists. Was the name-calling going to start all over again?

"Frau Luther!" Mother's new maidservant from nearby Coswig hurried up, worry lining her young, plump face. "I must talk to you."

"Yes? What is it?" Mother showed Lenchen a round cheese on the counter of a stall.

"It's your husband. He's sick," the maidservant panted, her eyes round with distress.

"Don't worry about it. It's just his way. He was all right when I left home." Mother asked the peasant woman the price of the cheese. The woman quoted a price that made Mother back off. "That's much more than we can pay," she told Lenchen.

"Frau Luther, your husband — " the maidservant ventured timidly.

"Oh, yes. You said he was sick, didn't you?" Mother turned to another stall and looked over the cheeses there. "He's probably working on a sermon, and you heard him groaning."

"Frau Luther, your husband is ill. Don't you even *care*?"

Hans smiled. When Father was really sick, Mother was right there nursing him back to health. Other times, when Father was worried or under pressure while preparing lectures, sermons, or answers to letters, he complained of aches and pains so much and so long that the whole family simply waited until he ran out of breath, and then Father would discover that he felt fine.

The new maidservant could not be expected to know Father's ways. She twisted her apron with nervous fingers. "He is all doubled up on the floor of the lecture hall."

For the first time, Mother looked alarmed. "Not in front of the students, I hope."

"No one is there, Frau Luther. He's all alone in that great big room. I heard him groaning, and — "

"Did he ask for me?"

"Frau Luther," the maidservant burst out, "how could he ask for anyone? He's *dying.*"

Mother cocked her head as if to hear better. "What makes you think so?"

"Frau Luther, he *said* so."

Mother sighed. "We'll never get our marketing done this way. Perhaps I'd better go home."

The maidservant wrung her hands. "Frau Luther, that's what I've been saying all the time." She rolled her eyes upward. "What kind of family is this?" Her voice rose, hysterically. "My family warned me. 'The Luthers,' they said, 'are different. They're not like other people.' But did I listen to my own family? No, and now I bitterly regret it. I've a good mind to go back to Coswig." She burst into tears and flung her white apron over her face.

Now Mother was really alarmed. "Don't say that, my good girl. We need you. The children need you. Come along with me. I'll tell you about Dr. Luther, and then you'll understand." She took money out of the little bag at her waist, spoke quickly to a stallkeeper about a cheese, and motioned to Hans. "Please carry the cheese home for me. Lenchen, you take Martin, and all of you come back home right away."

Mother hurried off, talking in her usual fast and earnest way to the new maidservant.

Hans hugged the cheese to his chest and started home with Lenchen and Martin. Because of Martin they had to walk slowly.

At the edge of the market square they came face-to-face with the three peasant boys.

"What's your name?" a dark-haired boy demanded.

"Hans. What's yours?"

"Blacky. What's her name?" Blacky jerked his head toward Lenchen.

"Magdalena," Lenchen said.

"Your mother called you *Lenchen*. How come?"

"It's her nickname," Little Martin blurted.

"Be quiet," his sister warned. "No one asked you, and don't tell your name."

"You'd better tell it." Blacky nodded toward the garbage-filled ditch. "You know what we could do to you? We could throw all three of you in there. How would you like that? So what is his name?"

"Martin Luther," little Martin blurted out.

"*Martin Luther!*" Blacky gasped. "That couldn't be your name. There's only one Martin Luther in Wittenberg, and my father says he ought to be run out of town."

"Martin Luther is my father," Martin explained innocently.

The three peasant boys looked at each other with sly grins. Blacky's eyes gleamed. "So you're the ones! You think you're smart because Martin Luther is your father." His mouth twisted in a sneer. "Imagine! A monk for a father and a nun for a mother. Monks and nuns aren't supposed to get married."

"Yeah," another boy chimed in. "Your parents can never go to heaven."

Lenchen gritted her teeth, clasped little Martin's hand, and pushed past the boys, her head high. "That's not true."

The three boys stepped in front of her with arms folded.

"Your father is nothing but a runaway monk," Blacky chanted.

"He is not."

"Yes, he is. And he married a runaway nun."

"He did not."

"Yes, he did, and your mother escaped from her convent in a big old fish barrel with some more nuns, and your house is nothing but an old broken-down monastery."

Little Martin burst into tears.

Lenchen comforted him. "You don't even know what a monastery is, so why are you crying?"

"I don't want to live in an old, broken-down monastery."

"It isn't broken down. Mother is having it all fixed up. Would you rather live here in the market square?"

"No." Martin cried louder than ever.

"Come on, Lenchen," Hans urged. "Don't pay

29

any attention to these boys." He hoped the bluff would work.

"I'm not moving until they get out of our way. They'll see that we're not afraid of them or anyone else."

Hans could have hugged Lenchen. His sister, always so calm and reasonable, would not let the peasant boys bully her.

A faraway clap of thunder hushed everyone in the market square. Stallkeepers hurriedly flung their wares into big sacks.

Blacky looked frightened. "It's the devil," he breathed. He and the other two boys turned quickly and ran off.

"The devil is loose," the stallkeepers told each other.

"Either that or it's Martin Luther preaching," a man called out. "Only his thunderstorms are in church."

Hans and Lenchen, with Martin between them, raced down the street toward the Black Cloister. Better a thunderstorm than a dip in the ditch!

A FIGHT FOR THE RIGHT

THE STORM had not broken yet, and Hans led the others to the Elster gate near the cemetery. "Let's stop and say hello to Elizabeth," he suggested.

Little Martin looked around. "Elizabeth who?"

"Our sister."

"Where is she?"

Hans pointed to a small gravestone set in the wall at the left of the entrance.

"What's she doing in there?"

"She's not there. She's in the cemetery, stupid."

"Don't say *stupid*, Hans," Lenchen chided.

"Why not? Father does. I've heard him call lots of people stupid, like the pope, Dr. Eck, Erasmus, Elector George, and — "

"That's enough."

Hans thought so, too. He didn't like to have Lenchen annoyed with him. She was the only one he could talk to. Their cousins were too old, and

31

Martin, Paul, and the baby were too young.

"What do those words say?" Martin asked.

Hans had studied Latin since he was four years old and he translated the plaque. "'Here sleeps Elizabeth, Martin Luther's little daughter, in the year 1528.'"

"Mother named Elizabeth after the mother of John the Baptist," Lenchen said.

"And she was born just after the pestilence in 1527," Hans added.

"Pest-i-lence?" Martin looked puzzled. "What's that?"

"It's the plague. People can be well one day and dead the next. No one knows who will get it and who won't. Lots of people leave town when it comes."

"Will there ever be another one?"

"No one knows that, either."

They started toward the Black Cloister. The rain still had not begun.

"Look! There's Blacky," Lenchen exclaimed. "He followed us."

Blacky swaggered up. Hans could see that his curiosity was stronger than the fear of the coming storm. "Do you live in that big building over there?" Blacky pointed to the four-storied Black Cloister rising above the walled courtyard.

"Yes."

"What's it like in there?"

"Oh, it's just a house." Hans knew Blacky had never seen a house like that, but Hans didn't want to brag.

"You think you're smart living in such a big

house. Your father has lots of enemies, and they all wish he was dead."

"Not anymore."

"Oh, yes they do. He's working hand in hand with the devil. My father says so. And your mother is nothing but a runaway nun."

That clinched it. Hans had heard more than enough. No one was going to say things like that about Mother and get away with it.

"Here, Lenchen. Hold the cheese." Hans pushed the cheese wheel toward her. Then he faced Blacky, but before he could duck, Blacky grabbed him around the neck and threw him to the ground. Hans wriggled loose and caught Blacky around the knees, pulling Blacky on top of him. Both boys rolled in the dirt, kicking and clawing. Neither one could gain an advantage.

Blacky's elbow caught Hans in the stomach. He gasped, pulled back, and heard a rip on the back of his short coat. Lenchen shrieked and shoved the cheese wheel into Blacky's ribs. He went over backward. Martin grabbed hold of Blacky's leg.

Rain pelted downward in a sudden burst drenching everyone and stopping the fight. Blacky sprang up, shook Martin off his leg, and for the second time that day ran away from the Luthers.

Hans' clothes were now muddy as well as torn. Blood dripped from his nose, but he looked at Lenchen in triumph. At least no one could say he was afraid to stand up for his family. He still burned, remembering Blacky's insulting remark about Mother.

Aunt Lena met the three Luther children at the passageway. At the sight of Hans, her eyebrows shot up. Without a word, she marched him to a washroom and sponged off his face. Her silence bothered Hans more than a scolding. He poured out the whole story. "I was fighting for what's right, Aunt Lena. Father does, so why can't I?"

"Because you lack self-control, young man. Your father doesn't want you to fight with peasants. It makes trouble for him in town. All his enemies are watching to see how he is bringing up his family. They're hoping his children will bring disgrace on him."

"But why?"

"It's a long story. Someday everything will be explained to you. Now, go dry your clothes by the fireplace before your father sees you. I'll mend your coat before your mother wonders what happened."

Hans sat before the fireplace and thought about what Aunt Lena had said. Everything he did — or did not do — could mean trouble for Father. Everyone he met might be a spy bringing ridicule to all the things for which Father had risked his life. People would laugh and say, "Look at this great man. He can't even bring up his own children to be an honor to him and to his church."

When Aunt Lena mended his coat, Hans pleaded, "You won't tell Mother about the fight, will you?"

"How about your father?"

"Oh, no, no. Please." Then Hans saw the twinkle in Aunt Lena's eyes. He laughed, too.

The heavy rain continued. The new maidservant ran back and forth with her hands over her ears. At last she cried out, "Where are your consecrated palm branches?"

34

"We don't have any," Aunt Lena said.

"Then how are we to keep the devil away?" the maidservant demanded. "Show me your holy water jug. I'll sprinkle the hearth and the fireplace."

"We don't have holy water."

The maidservant left, shaking her head and muttering to herself.

During the storm the Luthers gathered in the second-floor family room. Mother sat in the funny little raised seat by one window with her spinning wheel. Hans sat in the window seat of the other window. When he looked through the thick panes, even without rain, everything below wavered. Now with the rain, the trees and ground seemed to run together — like his own thoughts, Hans decided.

Mother murmured something to Father, sitting at the pine table across from her.

"Now, Kathe," Father began.

"All I said was, never ignore a thunderstorm," Mother laughed.

It was one of their secrets. *I'll ask Aunt Lena what it means,* Hans thought.

"Ask Father about being a monk," Lenchen whispered.

"I'm afraid."

"When you were a baby, you weren't afraid to sing when Father was studying. Aunt Lena said even when Father scolded you for making too much noise, you sang anyway."

Hans remembered the story — how he sang more softly but kept looking at Father warily, and Father said that was the way people should look at God.

"Someone has to ask him if we're ever going to

find out about how Father married Mother, and I think we have a right to know."

Hans agreed, especially if they were going to hear insults all the time about their family. He tried to think how to word the question. Should he say, "Are nuns ever allowed to marry?" Or should he just make a statement like, "I thought nuns weren't supposed to marry anyone."

Little Martin solved the problem. He blurted out in a loud voice, "Father, what's a monk?"

At first Father looked surprised. Then he snapped, "Monks are fleas on God Almighty's fur coat."

"Today someone said you married a nun, Father," Lenchen said.

Father looked at Mother, then back to Lenchen. "Yes, that's true."

"But I thought nuns couldn't marry," Hans broke in. "Don't they take vows to pray all the time? So how could they marry anyone?"

Father smiled at Mother. "Well, this one did."

"Is it true Mother was a runaway nun?" Hans asked. There, it was out.

"Yes. That is true also."

Hans took a deep breath. He hadn't expected Father to answer so simply. In fact, he had thought Father might explode in anger, the way he sometimes did, except that Father liked being married to Mother. Everyone knew that.

Father cleared his throat. "Ask your Aunt Lena about these things. She knows the whole story."

At bedtime, Hans and Lenchen asked Aunt Lena how Father met Mother.

Aunt Lena pursed her lips, but settled on a

stool and smoothed her long skirts. "It's a long story."

At the word *story* Martin and even little Paul clamored to hear. "Tell us, tell us," they begged.

"When your mother was only ten years old she was put in the convent at Nimbschen."

"Did she want to go?" Martin asked.

"Yes and no. I was already there. Your grandfather had married again after your grandmother died, so it seemed best to have her in the convent with me."

"Did you pray a lot?" Lenchen asked.

"Yes, we did, and we still do."

"Did Mother marry Jesus?"

Aunt Lena smiled. "That was a way of saying that nuns are more concerned with glorifying God than having a family. We had been in the convent a long time and we began reading books by a certain Martin Luther."

"That's Father," Martin exclaimed.

"Yes. He had been a monk for almost twenty years, but he was not satisfied with the way the church took money and then said people's sins were forgiven. He believed God alone could forgive sins, and that God would guide those who believed in Him."

"Is that why Mother ran away?"

"Yes. She and I and ten others fled."

"In fish barrels?"

Aunt Lena laughed and laughed. "Not exactly. We were all humped down in a wagon and a big cloth was thrown over us."

"What would have happened if you'd been discovered?" Hans asked.

37

Aunt Lena tightened her lips. "Well, we were in Duke George's territory and he had a man executed who tried to help some other nuns to escape. But we were fortunate. Our driver was Leonard Koppe. He was about sixty years old and had brought many barrels of smoked herring to the convent and took the empties back again."

"So when all of you were humped down you looked like empty fish barrels?" Lenchen asked.

"That's right," Aunt Lena answered. "The Tuesday after Easter nine of us were in Wittenberg, still dressed in our nun's habits and without money. Your father wrote to people how sorry he was for us. We were a wretched little bunch, he said. And that's how your father met your mother."

"Why do they joke about thunderstorms?" Hans asked.

"That's another story."

"Tell us, tell us."

"When your father was a student at the University of Erfurt, he was walking down a road and there was a big thunderstorm. A ball of lightning struck near him."

"Was he scared?" Martin asked.

"He certainly was. So much so that he begged Saint Anne to spare his life. If she would, he vowed to become a monk."

"And she did, and he did," Martin said.

"But I thought when you were a monk you got locked up and never, never got out again," Hans said. "So how could Father quit being a monk?"

"He didn't want to quit, but he could see so many things going wrong in the church that he wrote

38

and spoke about it. More and more people believed what he was saying, and the pope had him excommunicated."

"Ex — ex — " Martin could not get the big word out. "What does that mean?"

"It means you aren't part of the church anymore," Aunt Lena said.

"So then he had to make a new church."

"He hadn't intended to do that at all. He just wanted to correct the things that were wrong, but people started breaking away from the Catholic Church, and that is how the re-forming of the church started."

No wonder Father was so important, Hans thought. He had started all those changes.

"Aunt Lena, read us the letter Father wrote to Hans from Coburg that time." Lenchen brought out the letter from a chest of drawers.

"You mean Gruboc?" Aunt Lena's eyes twinkled. Hans knew there was some joke.

"No, Coburg." Lenchen was certain about that.

"Your father called it *Gruboc*," Aunt Lena explained. "That's *Coburg* spelled backward. You know your father is always joking. Here's the letter. Let's see. Hans was about the age of Martin when the letter was written." She began to read. "To my dearest son, Hänschen Luther in Wittenberg: Mercy and peace in Christ, beloved son. I am glad to hear that you are studying hard and praying earnestly. Continue, my little son. When I come I'll bring you a very nice gift.

"I know of a beautiful garden where many children play. They wear golden robes and pick up

39

beautiful apples, pears, cherries, and plums from under the trees. They sing, prance around, and are very happy. They have a beautiful little horse with gold bridle and silver saddle. I asked the owner of the garden whose children these were. He said they were children who like to pray, to read, and who are devout.

"I said, 'Dear man, I have a son whose name is Hänschen Luther. Could he come to this garden, eat these beautiful apples and pears, ride the handsome little horse, and play with these children?'

"The man said, 'If he likes to pray, to read, and is devout, then he will be welcome in this garden. Lippus and Jost can come, too, and when they all get here, there will be whistles, drums, lutes, and harps. There will also be dancing and shooting with little crossbows.'

"Then he showed me a beautiful meadow in the garden ready for dancing, with golden pipes, drums, and silver crossbows hanging there. But it was still early and the children had not eaten yet, and because of this I could not wait for the dancing. I said to the man, 'Oh, dear sir, I want to go quickly and write all of this to my dear little son Hans, so that he will continue to learn and pray and be devout. Then he can come into this garden. But he also has an Aunt Lena, and she has to be here with him.'

"The man said, 'She can come, too. Go ahead and write to him.'

"Because of this, dear little son Hans, learn and pray and be of good cheer. Tell Lippus and Jost about this so that they also will learn and pray.

40

In this way all of you will come into this garden. With this I commend you to the almighty God. Greet Aunt Lena from me with a kiss. Your loving father, Martin Luther."

Hans had heard the letter many times, and each time he wondered if he were learning enough, praying enough, and becoming devout enough. Trying to study in the Black Cloister was hard. The older cousins living there talked noisily. The little children, Martin and Paul, scampered down the long halls on their wooden horses, laughing and shouting. Visitors came in and out. The hired help talked at their work. People came to sell wood, or buy or bargain over the cattle Mother had bought.

All the people there seemed to know what they were doing and why. *All except me,* Hans thought. He loved to hear Father's letter read aloud, but he was beginning to wish he could always remain as young as the Hans in the letter.

While Aunt Lena put the younger children to bed, Lenchen remarked how nice it would be not to have to grow up.

"But you don't have anything to worry about," Hans said. "Boys have to *be* something when they grow up. Girls just stay around the house."

"Mother doesn't just stay around the house. She works in the garden and takes care of the fishpond and the cows and pigs and geese."

"Well, I can't just have a garden and a pond and some cows and geese. I have to *be* something. Can't you see what I mean?"

"Oh," Lenchen said, "you mean like a lawyer or preacher?"

"Yes." The worries about *being* something started up all over again. "I can't be as famous as Father. I can't start a Reformation. He's already done it. And I can't even fight for a right cause, like I tried to do today, because people will criticize Father for not having a family who obeys him."

How strange it all seemed. To think that a fight for the right could be wrong!

A WEDDING SUPPER

THE NEXT day after his Latin lesson, Hans curled up on the window seat of the family room reading a fable by Aesop, translated into German by his father. Martin and Paul played in one corner. Lenchen ran in with a big smile.

"Guess what Mother just told me. She almost wasn't our mother."

"What do you mean?"

"She almost married a rich man, only when he went back to his hometown he married someone else. Father had arranged marriages for other nuns, and he wanted Mother to marry Dr. Glatz, and she wouldn't. She said she would marry either Dr. Amsdorf or Father himself, so then Father married Mother. And guess what else."

"Well, what?"

"Sometimes when Father writes to that rich man he sends friendly greetings from 'his old flame.' Isn't that funny? And sometimes Father sends greetings

43

to people like this: 'From me and my rib to you and your rib and all the little ribs." Lenchen burst out laughing. "Father is so funny."

But Father didn't always joke. When he came to the family room later, after Mother had come in to spin, he slumped in his chair before the pine table.

"There has been nobody in a thousand years whom the world hates so much as me."

"Oh, Doctor, don't say such things," Mother exclaimed.

Father went right on. "It's said that in Rome the word *reformation* is hated more than thunder or the last judgment."

"Well, Doctor, after all, you have made a thunderstorm in church."

Father's chuckle was half groan. "That's true, and they'll have more trouble with a dead Luther than a thousand living ones. I'm fed up with the world, Kathe, and it is fed up with me. It won't be long before the world sees me no more."

"See to it, sir, that you don't imagine things."

"Oh, I won't die suddenly. First I'll lie down and be sick."

"You work too hard," Mother said.

Father disagreed. "These headaches and stomach pains — they're not because I work too hard. They are Satan's attacks." He rested his head on one hand. "Nobody believes me when I complain about the painful ringing and buzzing in my ears. It's just like three years ago. I can't even sit down and read for an hour. The ringing begins and I'm forced to lie down. Still, I don't want to find fault with my head. It has faithfully ventured into

44

battle with me. It deserves my best thanks."

That was like Father. No matter what complaints he had, he joked about them sooner or later. "Christians should be happy and cheerful," he always said.

When he felt better, Mother reminded him of a wedding supper they were going to give for one of his students. "Doctor, we simply must be more careful about furnishing gifts and wedding suppers for your students."

Father held up his hand with the fingers spread. "God divided the hand into fingers so that money can slip through," he laughed. "Whatever we give away, God will give back to us."

He looked over a pile of bills and groaned. "We have pigs, cows, calves, a goat, chickens, and geese. Aren't they worth money? Can't we sell them and pay our bills, Herr Kathe?"

Father always called Mother *Herr* Kathe, as if she were a man, when household problems came up. He knew nothing about the actual details of running a house. Fortunately Mother had learned to manage such things during the two years she stayed with the Cranach family before her marriage.

"We can't sell anything at a moment's notice, Doctor. We have to think of the future."

Father sighed. "These household affairs trouble me. What a child I am in such things! I never did like keeping money accounts. It depresses me. It always comes out short."

"We have to deal with these matters some way," Mother said.

45

"Yes," Father agreed. "If I prick my finger, my whole body feels it." He reminded Mother that once his income was less than nine guilders. When he married, it was increased to one hundred guilders and doubled again after that. Father accepted no lecture fees from university students, and refused to take money for his published writings. "Tell me, Herr Kathe, where is the money to come from?"

Little Martin, playing in the corner, must have heard the word *money*. "Look in the money drawer, Father."

Father took out a key and unlocked the drawer of the pine table. "Empty!" he exclaimed. Then he recited a little poem:

> *"Is there any poor wretch keeps house so ill?*
> *For when I need money to pay a bill*
> *And look for it in the place I know*
> *Not a penny is there*
> *Though I search high and low."*

"We'll manage some way," Mother said cheerfully.

"I don't manage figures very well," Father said. "I can't understand them. I was never taught arithmetic. I know I spend far more than I get from my salary. Still," he added with conviction, "he who has Christ and the Scripture has enough." He smiled at Mother. "By the way, Kathe, you have done so well on your Bible reading, I hope you keep it up."

"I've read enough. I've heard enough. I know enough. Would to God I lived it," Mother said tartly.

46

When the dining room was almost filled, Father played his lute and everyone sang.

"Now, Kathe, that's how people begin to stray from the Word of God."

"Don't worry. I'll stick to Christ like a burr to a topcoat," Mother laughed.

A few days later Father received a marriage announcement from one of his students. "Another wedding supper means another gift," he told Mother. "Will we have to pawn one of our two silver goblets, Kathe? We must give if we would have."

Father and Mother had received the goblets as a wedding present when they were married.

This time Mother had good news. "Some of the students have paid for their board, so we have enough for a gift and the supper, too."

Little Martin and Paul ran in to tell of a wedding parade they had seen passing down the street. Hans saw Mother and Father exchange smiles. It dawned on him that *they* had done this, too. Imagine! Mother and Father on a two-wheeled cart drawn by people instead of horses, with flute players leading the parade all over town.

When the time came for the wedding supper, Hans and Lenchen waited in the courtyard with Father for the guests and wedding couple to arrive. Some startled birds flew from their nest in a nearby tree.

"Little birds, don't fly away," Father said. "I wish you nothing but good. If only you'd believe me." He added, "This is how we should believe God — that He wishes us well with His whole heart."

When everyone had come, the dining hall was almost filled. Father played his lute and everyone sang. Later, a guest teased Father about a monk marrying.

"My enemies will not forgive my marriage," Father told the guests. Everyone at any meal always listened when Father talked. "They joke about it every day. When I got married, the world laughed, but Kathe was worth more to me than the entire kingdom of France."

He told how at the Wartburg Castle, in a friendly prison where his enemies could not get to him, messengers had brought news that the monks in Wittenberg were marrying. "And I said, 'What! Will our Wittenbergers give wives to monks? They won't give one to me.'"

Everyone laughed.

"It was Argula von Grumbach who urged me to seal my testimony by marrying," Father continued. "I refused."

"Why was that?" a guest asked.

"Because I expected daily to suffer the death of a heretic."

"What persuaded you to marry?"

"In June 1525, I heard that Albert, the Archbishop of Mainz, against whom the ninety-five theses were directed, was thinking of marrying. I wrote that if my own marriage would be an encouragement, I was ready. I knew my marriage would please my father, rile the pope, make angels laugh and devils weep."

A guest spoke up. "Did you know that Erasmus saw a change in you six months later? He said, 'Luther begins to be milder; he doesn't rage so with his pen. Nothing is so wild that a female won't tame it.'"

Everyone burst out laughing. Mother, too.

Father chuckled. "Man has strange thoughts the first year of marriage. Sitting at the table, he thinks, 'Before, I was alone. Now there are two.' "

He smiled as if to himself. "Wives ask their busy husbands lots of unimportant little things. My Kathe used to sit next to me with her spinning at first while I was trying to study hard. She'd ask a question like, 'Is the Minister of Prussia the brother of the Margrave?' I didn't think it possible that someone wouldn't know that. I thought Kathe asked me just to have something to say."

"That's unjust," Mother defended herself. "How should I know such things? I was put in the convent when I was ten, and politics were never discussed. When I married, my head spun from all the new things I had to learn. I couldn't sort out the many princes of the Holy Roman Empire."

"Where would we be if it were not for women?" Father laughed. "Sometimes I tease Kathe. I tell her the Old Testament says a man can have more than one wife."

"And I always tell the Doctor I'd desert him and the children and go back to the cloister." Mother had left the silence of the cloister far behind. Now she spoke freely, at the same time seeing to it that the small details of running a house were kept from bothering Father.

"It's the greatest blessing of God when love continues to flower in marriage," Father went on. "There is no sweeter union than that of a happy marriage. Children are the fruit and joy of marriage, of which the pope is not worthy."

"I heard you put it another way," a guest spoke

up. "You said a child is the best wool that one can shear from the sheep."

The smiling wedding guests agreed.

"How strange that the love of the parents grows greater and stronger when the child needs their care more," Father mused. "I remember with Martin, the loving, patient way in which Kathe took care of him. She surrounded him with loving words when he didn't deserve them. It reminded me of God's patience and mercy. I remember, too, when Kathe and Aunt Lena wanted to dress the baby. He fought against it with hands and feet. I said then, 'Scream and defend yourself. The pope has also tied me up, but I am free now.'"

The wedding supper continued with much talking and laughing. When it was time for bed, Hans suggested, "Let's play monastery."

"All right," Lenchen agreed. "Now, no one can talk or laugh."

The children all lined up, put their hands up their sleeves and looked at the floor. They climbed the steep, winding stairs to the top floor. Aunt Lena followed with baby Margarete.

"What was Father before he married Mother?" Martin asked.

"A monk, stupid," Hans answered.

"Hans, don't use that word!" Lenchen said.

"What do monks do?"

"They sit in their cells and read the Bible and pray all day long."

"What do their families do?"

"They don't have families."

"Is Father a monk now?" Martin asked.

51

"Of course not, stu — "

"Hans!" Lenchen put both hands on her hips and glared at Hans. "That's a terrible word."

Martin kept on with his questions. "Then why does Father sit in his cell and read the Bible and pray?"

Hans groaned in exasperation. Aunt Lena hugged Martin and explained Father's work.

"Why is he sick so much?"

Aunt Lena explained that Father worked so hard at being a monk he lost his health. Like the other monks, Father prayed seven times a day. If he missed for some reason, he made up the time, exhausting himself. He fasted longer than he had to.

"Will Father go to heaven?" Martin asked.

Aunt Lena smiled. "Your father always said if any monk ever got to heaven through monkery, then he too should have made it."

Lenchen wanted to hear more about Father marrying Mother.

Aunt Lena laughed aloud. "Your father's friends were astonished. They said, 'For heaven's sake, not this one!' "

Hans was shocked. How could anyone criticize Mother? But of course the peasant woman at the marketplace did, and there must be others, especially those who did not approve of Father.

"When your father decided to marry, he acted quickly. He told a friend, 'Don't put off until tomorrow. By delay Hannibal lost Rome. By delay Esau forfeited his birthright. Christ said, 'You shall seek me and not find me.' Thus Scripture, experience, and all creation testify that the gifts of

52

God must be taken on the wing."

"When was that?" Lenchen asked.

"June 10. On June 13, 1525, he publicly announced that he would marry your mother, and in the eyes of the law, he was at that moment a married man."

The idea of law interested Hans. Father always obeyed the law. Why didn't he like lawyers?

"Because lawyers don't give anything to God but only to themselves," Aunt Lena said briskly. "Now, don't bother your father with questions about them. As he says, he is a shepherd of souls, not of bodies."

"What else did Father do?" Martin asked. "I mean, before we were born."

But Aunt Lena said the children had talked enough for one night.

"Tell us something at bedtime every night about Father, will you, Aunt Lena?" Lenchen begged.

"Yes, do," the others chorused.

Hans hoped she would. There weren't many men in the world like Father.

A TIMELY RESCUE

THE NEXT day Hans heard Tölpel bark and went to the outside passageway to see what was the matter. No one was in sight, except Martin, huddled in a corner with the dog.

"What are you doing hiding there? And with the dog?" Hans asked.

"I'm just petting him."

"But why in a dark corner? Let's go out in the courtyard. Tölpel's making too much noise."

Outside, Martin slumped on a stone bench. Tölpel, with drooping tail, waited until Hans told him to lie down.

"Martin, what's the matter with Tölpel? Did he eat something that didn't agree with him?"

"I guess so."

Lenchen hurried out. "Did anyone see a letter for Father? A messenger left one, and it has disappeared. I found some scraps of paper in the passageway, but of course that couldn't be the letter."

"Father gets so many letters he could fill a big room with them. He said so. So what's one more letter?" Martin asked.

"It has the names of some preachers who are coming here."

"If the letter is lost, how did Father know it came?" Hans asked.

"Because the messenger came back for an answer. Did you see it?"

"No."

"Did you, Martin?"

Little Martin hung his head still lower. "No," he mumbled.

"You're acting so odd," Lenchen exclaimed. "I don't think you're telling the truth. Stop patting Tölpel." Lenchen took the dog's head between her hands. Martin looked away. "What's that black stuff on your hands, Martin? Why, it's ink. Now I know what those scraps were that I found. Tölpel chewed up the letter. Martin, you were teasing him with it, weren't you?"

"Maybe."

"Martin, you'll have to tell Father what happened."

Martin jumped up in alarm. "Oh, no, Lenchen. Don't make me."

"Father forgives people who confess, just as God does. You'll have to go." She gave him a little shove.

"Well, I'm going to take Tölpel. He's got to confess, too."

In a little while Martin came back with a big smile. Tölpel was wagging his tail. "Father forgave us both. He says God tells us He is going to punish us, but if we will cry and run to Him, He will rescue us and comfort us. But Father didn't even punish Tölpel and me."

Later, Lippus Melanchthon and Jost Jonas came over to play. Hans told his friends about the letter.

"Then let's have a disputation," Lippus promptly said.

"What's that?" Martin was suspicious.

"Well, it's where you have two sides. One side argues for something and the other against it. There's an officer in charge to keep people from fighting," Lippus explained. "Your father has been in lots of them."

They all went to the empty lecture hall. There was a table with elaborate carvings at one end for those who would do the arguing, and a tall chair for the officer in charge. Lippus sat in that chair because he was the oldest. After Jost questioned Martin in a corner of the hall, he and Hans took their places behind the table below Lippus.

"Master Martinus, step forward," Lippus said.

Martin did not move.

"Martinus, hurry up," Hans said.

"Do you mean me?"

"Yes. Who else?"

"But that isn't my name."

"Yes, it is. It's the Latin form."

"Oh." Martin stood in front of Lippus.

Motioning with his hands, Jost began his plea. "Martinus Luther, the Younger, claims that the dog Tölpel did jump upon him when he was handed a letter by a messenger. Said dog barked and yipped. Aunt Lena von Bora came along with

56

Margarete and Paul Luther, both crying, and besought the said Martinus to take said dog out of the house. There was too much noise already, she claimed, what with students coming in and out, servants running back and forth doing their work, and babies crying. To coax said dog, Martinus dangled the letter in front of Tölpel's nose. Tölpel thought it was play and wrestled with said Martinus Luther, the Younger. In so doing, the letter was torn to pieces. My defendant is innocent. I rest my case."

Then it was Hans' turn. "This dog Tölpel is famous for his mischievous tricks."

Lenchen laughed. "I thought this was a disputation."

Lippus pounded his gavel. "Women have to be quiet."

"Mother isn't," Lenchen began, but stopped when Hans glared at her.

"Said dog Tölpel, being one of God's lower creatures," Hans continued, "could not withstand the natural order of things and did seize and chew the letter. My father says, 'You don't tell a pig "You must eat," for it eats without being bidden. An apple tree bears fruit without my telling it to.' Therefore, a dog will chew letters if given the chance. It is not a matter of right or wrong. It's just his nature."

A feeling of triumph welled up in Hans. He enjoyed speaking at the mock trial. *Maybe I'll study law someday,* he thought, and pushed back a twinge of guilt. Father didn't like lawyers. Disputation, according to him, was only threshing empty straw.

"Who had the best argument?" Lippus asked.

Lenchen voted for Hans. Martin voted for Jost.

"Very well. The case is closed." Lippus banged Father's gavel on the lectern, stepped down, and shook hands with Martin. Tölpel wagged his tail.

Students started coming into the lecture hall. It was almost time for one of Father's classes. Hans let the others to the courtyard. They sat on a stone bench near the water pump.

"Your father doesn't have to pay any tax on water, does he?" Jost asked Hans.

Lippus answered for him. "No, and neither does my father. They're famous."

"What does that have to do with paying a water tax?" Jost asked.

"Because hundreds of students have come here to study with my father and Hans' father. The students have to eat and sleep and buy things. The shopkeepers are happy. The innkeepers are happy. Everybody is happy. The town council decided no more water tax for us or for the Luthers."

"I'll bet the council didn't like it when the people used to cross the border into Saxony and spend their money on indulgences," Jost said. "They did it even when they were going to your father's church," he told Hans with a sly smile.

Hans knew enough about indulgences to know that Father did not like them, but he wasn't at all sure how people bought them or what they got for their money. He did not want to show his ignorance before Jost. "Oh, Father knew all about that."

"No, he didn't, or he wouldn't have let them stay in his church," Jost retorted. "My father told me all about it. Those people would go look at a hair of Mary's head, or a piece of straw from the manger, or some bread from the Last Supper. Then they paid money and their sins were all forgiven."

Hans' curiosity overcame him. "How did they buy indulgences?"

Jost swelled with importance. "First there was a procession, with a big cross. The indulgence letter was carried on a velvet cushion with lots of gold embroidery on it. Someone would tell people to put money in the coffer and then their dead relatives would be released from purgatory. My father told me all about it."

"*My* father told people if they were sorry for their sins, they didn't have to pay any money," Lenchen said.

"Just the same, some people have done it," Jost insisted.

That night at bedtime Hans asked Aunt Lena why some people thought they could pay to have their sins forgiven.

"There will always be some people who believe they can pay for God's favor," Aunt Lena said, "but it was on exactly that point that the pope became angry with your father." She told how Father had written out ninety-five ideas about why indulgences were wrong. He had them printed on a large sheet of heavy paper. Then, about noon on October 31, 1517, he and a companion walked to the castle church and posted the paper on the door.

"What does *posted* mean?" Martin asked.

"He took a big hammer and a nail," Lenchen told him.

"And he pounded and he pounded on the old church door," Martin sang happily.

Aunt Lena told how the pope called Father a wild boar and ordered that his books be burned. On December 10, 1520, Father and some students threw a letter from the pope into a bonfire in front of Elster gate. Then the students held a parade with a trumpeter blowing loud blasts. The next day in the lecture room, with over three hundred people present, Father spoke German instead of Latin and said he hadn't meant for them to have a demonstration. "Your father didn't like to see students do things like that."

She told how excited people became over Father's ideas of faith in God. Everything Father wrote was published by printer after printer in various cities. People read, thought, and discussed Father's ideas. Church officials called Father a heretic. They wanted to burn him at the stake, like other martyrs. But Father had many influential friends. They demanded that any charges had to be presented in an orderly way, through disputations.

"That's what Father did at Worms," Hans said.

"Yes. The church officials wanted him to take back everything he had been writing and preaching. In the spring of 1521, your father entered Worms, guarded by one hundred horsemen. People crowded the streets that afternoon and even climbed on roofs to watch your father arrive for the meeting. Inside the building Spaniards, Italians, Danes, Poles, Hungarians, and a French envoy waited, as well as an English ambassador."

"Did they all know about Father?" Lenchen asked.

In December 1520 Father and some students threw a letter from the pope into a bonfire in front of Elster gate.

Aunt Lena nodded. "Your father's books had been heaped on a bench. He had to answer two questions: 'Do you here publicly admit that you wrote these books? Do you still believe what you wrote, or do you confess you were wrong?' "

"What did Father say?" the children chorused together.

"First, he quoted from the Bible, 'Whosoever shall deny me before men, him will I also deny before my Father which is in heaven.' Then he said he needed time to answer the next question. They gave him until the next day, when he came back. The torches were already lit."

"What for?" Hans asked.

"For the procession. Everyone expected him to admit he was wrong, but when the official asked him if he wished to confess, your father said, "Show me my error from the prophets and the gospels. Correct me from these and I will gladly confess my error and be the first to cast my writings into the fire."

"What did they say?"

"They refused to discuss the Bible with him."

"And then?"

"Your father said, 'Unless I am convicted from the Scriptures, because I cannot believe either the pope or the council alone, I am bound by my conscience and the Word of God. Therefore, I can and will confess no error, because to act against one's conscience is neither safe nor sound.' "

"Now comes the exciting part," Hans said. He had heard many houseguests talk about what happened next.

62

"The church officials wanted to condemn your father, but they were afraid the common people would start a riot, so they told your father to go home. On the way, a group of armed horsemen dashed out of the woods near Eisenach and surrounded the wagon."

"And then they dragged Father out — " Hans said.

"Let Aunt Lena tell it," Lenchen insisted.

"Your father snatched up his Hebrew Bible and his Greek New Testament. The horsemen cursed him and made him run alongside the horses. When they were out of sight of the wagon and the other people, the men gave your father a horse to ride. They traveled for many hours up a winding road to Wartburg Castle. The drawbridge was lowered. Hans von Berlepsch, the captain of the castle, received him. Your father was taken to two small rooms which could be entered only by a ladder. At night the ladder was removed. Your father grew a beard to disguise himself. He was known as Junker Jörg, guest of the castle. Of course he couldn't wear his monk's robes. Instead, he wore the clothing of a knight."

"And he stayed there until he translated the Bible," Hans said. "Nobody saw him except the page boys who brought him his meals."

Martin was staring at Aunt Lena and Hans with sorrowful eyes. "Didn't anyone like Father?"

"They *did* like him. That's why they put him in a safe place so none of his enemies could hurt or kill him," Aunt Lena explained. "You see, notices had gone out that no one was to help him, or give him food. Anyone who did would be fined heavily.

So that's why your father's friends put him in the castle."

The story excited Martin so much that he jumped on his wooden horse and ran circles around little Paul explaining that he was going to rescue him. Paul burst into tears.

Hans remembered another time when one of the children had cried for a long time. Father had said, "What have you done that I should love you so? You have disturbed the whole household with your bawling."

On another occasion when the children had quarreled then made up, Father said, "Dear God, how pleased You must be with the life and play of such children. All their sins are nothing else than forgiveness of sins."

When Hans slipped into bed that night, he recalled hearing once how Father, before his marriage, had gone a whole year without making his bed. His straw mattress had rotted. But life at the Black Cloister was different now. Mother had rescued Father just in time!

AN INVISIBLE ENEMY

IN THE lecture hall of the Black Cloister, Father's afternoon was well under way. In a small study room on another floor, Hans hunched over his Latin lesson. His tutor, Jerome Weller, a shy, withdrawn young man, dozed by the window.

Hans wrote the last word of his Latin lesson with a triumphant flourish of the pen. Herr Weller should be pleased this time. Hans had finished faster than usual, in spite of the noise on all four floors. Of course, no one expected students, guests, the older cousins, Hans' two sisters and two brothers — to say nothing of the hired help — to be silent from morning to night. After all, the Black Cloister was no longer a quiet monastery.

Today, Hans became aware of another kind of noise out in the hall. Was Father's lecture already over? Students often stayed afterward for private discussions, sometimes going into an empty room and talking over the ideas Father had brought out in his lecture. This time the voices sounded different, high and strained.

There was a shuffle, a grunt, a gasp; bumps, thumps, and a blood-curdling groan. Hans jumped up, pushed back his sloped study desk, and saw too late that the ink bottle had splashed over his paper. Maybe that was the devil's doing. That was the way Father always talked. Father said he'd thrown his inkwell at the devil once, but Hans was never sure whether Father meant he actually did, or whether the words he wrote in ink were what he threw to scare the devil away.

Hans wasn't sure what to do next. Should he copy his lesson over, and avoid a scolding from Herr Weller, or should he find out what was happening?

The thumps and groans continued. Hans' breath quickened. His hair prickled at the back of his neck. Was someone being murdered out there? Or was it possible that the devil was trying to lure him outside? Hans had never before thought of the devil as that real. Father's devil always seemed to bother only Father, somehow.

Hans looked at his tutor. Herr Weller was still asleep with one leg tucked under him on the window seat and his head on his arm. It wouldn't hurt to take a peek outside, Hans thought, and tiptoed to the door.

Instantly, Herr Weller woke. His feet hit the floor. "What is it?"

"An — an unusual noise. May I see what it is?"
"I hear no noise."

It started again. *Bump, slide, groan, bump, bump, groan.*

66

"I can't imagine — " Herr Weller began, still dazed from his nap.

"May I go see? Here is my lesson." Hans thrust the smudged assignment into Herr Weller's hands and slipped outside.

In the dark hallway, two students dragged a third between them. The third student's feet dragged, making curious bumps and scraping noises.

The first student leaned against the wall and panted, "Caspar, what are we going to do? We can't go on this way."

"Maybe it's not what you think," Caspar said.

"I know the symptoms. After all, it was only eight years ago since — "

Caspar broke in. "Let's put him in a wagon and send him home."

"Where'll we get one?"

"Ask Dr. Luther."

"He's not through lecturing yet. Besides, we can't ask for his wagon. He needs it himself for his trips out of town."

Caspar eased the sick student to a sitting position. "We can't stay here. Let's find some of the hired help."

"Oh, no, we can't do that. The news would spread all over town in no time."

Caspar thought a moment. "Well, then, can't we hoist him up and pretend he's drunk? That wouldn't be too strange here at the Black Cloister. I understand one of Dr. Luther's nephews gets drunk pretty often."

"The sooner we get out of here, the better for us, and for Wittenberg, too," the first student sighed.

"Do you really think it's the — "

"Be quiet. Don't even mention the word. Think of what happened at the university the last time. Almost everyone fled."

Caspar made one last try. "Can't we get Frau Luther? I have heard that she is as good as a doctor of medicine herself."

"No, we can't. There are little ones here. They might catch it."

Hans listened, at first completely baffled. Then an inkling of truth dawned. Should he let himself be seen? Should he go downstairs and tell Mother? Or should he interrupt his father in the lecture hall? No, he couldn't do that. Mother would know best what to do.

Hans started down the hall.

"What are you doing here?" the first student asked in an angry whisper.

"I just came out to see what was going on." Hans looked at the sick student slumped on the floor like a pile of limp clothes. Then Hans saw the staring eyes, the mouth an open O of pain.

"Who are you?" Caspar demanded.

"Hans Luther."

Both students groaned.

"Can you keep a secret?" Caspar asked.

"Yes, but — "

"You mustn't tell anyone, least of all your father."

"What's the matter with — with him?" Hans faltered, dreading to hear the word.

"Shall we tell him?" the first student asked.

"No, no," Caspar hissed. "Let's go."

They hoisted the sick student between them and

At the entrance of the university, a group of students talked
in hushed tones. A death cart rumbled past.

made their way to the lower floor. Hans followed. To his relief, Mother came in from the garden.

"Oh, what's the matter?" Mother ran to help.

"Frau Luther, one of the students has become ill, and we're taking him back to his room."

Always hospitable, Mother asked, "Don't you want to leave him here? We have plenty of rooms available."

"No, thank you, Frau Luther," Caspar replied. "It would be better if he went home."

"Then go with them," Mother told Hans. "Let me know how he is."

Hans followed the students down the main street of Wittenberg. At the entrance of the university, a group of students talked in hushed tones. A death cart rumbled out past the students. Hans glimpsed a covered figure behind the driver's seat. He was more certain than ever about what was happening. To his relief, he found his friends Lippus and Jost huddled near the wall watching.

"What's happening?" Hans demanded.

"Can't you guess?" Lippus asked.

"The plague?" Hans whispered. The last siege had been in 1527, when Hans was only two.

"Yes. How dreadful! I hope we don't get it."

The news spread fast over the town. People kept indoors. The outbreak was not as severe as earlier ones, but everyone lived in terror. A black cross was placed on the door of houses where a plague victim lived.

Friends advised Father to flee. He was too important to risk death from the plague.

"Where would I go?" Father demanded. "The

world would not fall to pieces if I died."

He ministered to the sick in the firm belief that God would protect him. Only once did he become upset. He had prayed with two women in the home of Bartholomew Schadewalk, a town councilman. "When I came home," Hans heard Father telling friends, "I took hold of my Margarete's face with my unwashed hands. I wasn't thinking. Otherwise I wouldn't have done it, for it tempts God." He mentioned two university students who had died. One was the sick student Hans had seen. "One day healthy and the next day buried." Father shook his head. "The plague strikes cruelly and suddenly, especially the younger generation."

Friends continued to advise the Luthers to leave Wittenberg.

"We'll stay where we are needed," Mother said.

It was strange, Hans thought. Mother was more afraid of the dreaded Turks attacking Wittenberg than of the plague, and more calm than when the maidservant from Coswig left.

Father was upset about that, too. "A maidservant should think of her place in life and of her work as holy," he declared.

He was even more upset when one of Hans' cousins came home drunk. "Drink until misfortune overtakes you," he roared. Later, he burst out, "He knows I and my family are spied on with lynx eyes from all sides! He knows that my enemies have such a sharp smell their noses reach from Rome to Wittenberg! If I had ten virtues and only one fault, people would talk about my one fault and never mention the ten virtues. How can I tell our

71

preachers the words of the Apostle Paul, 'A bishop should be a man who takes good care of his house and does a good job of bringing up his children?' How can I tell the pastors that their lives should be blameless in the face of their enemies and without offense to their friends, without even a shadow of suspicion? To think that my nephew would come in drunk!"

Still, Father understood the invisible enemy and knew how to combat him. "The devil hates music," Father said. "He cannot endure gaiety." In the evenings, Father played his lute and everyone sang.

To persons trying hard to live as Christians, he advised, "Don't always wrestle with the devil. Don't argue with him. He has had five thousand years of experience. He has tried out all his tricks on Adam, Abraham, and David, and he knows your weak spots. Seek company," he would say. "Eve got into trouble when she walked in the garden alone. Joke and sing. Make yourself eat. Fasting is the worst thing you can do when you are tempted."

Father admitted the devil had his uses. "When the devil brings bad thoughts into our heads against our will, and in spite of our struggle against them, God wishes to occupy us so that we don't get lazy and snore but fight against them and pray."

Father always prayed with the whole household before meals, and taught the children during worship times. "Young people must be brought up to learn the Scriptures," he said.

When Father was away, Mother instructed the children from a small catechism Father had prepared. Mother called the little book *Kattegissema,* and she smiled when she said the word. Hans knew it was a mixture of Greek and Latin and somehow a joke on Mother's name of *Kathe*. "Everything your father ever said is in this little book," Mother told Hans and the others.

Father did not instruct merely by words. Sometimes he punished the children with a switch cut from a young tree.

"Father hit Cousin Andreas with a switch," Hans told Lenchen once.

"Why?"

"He caught him saying a bad word," Hans explained.

"Boys are ruined through being too easy on them," he heard Father tell a houseguest. "They have to be brought up stricter. If father and mother don't judge, later the executioner has to judge."

Hans was quite aware that Father joked with Lenchen and not with him. But he did not mind. Everyone loved Lenchen.

Sometimes Lenchen puzzled Hans with her talk about heaven.

"I know more about it than you think I do," she announced one day.

"How could you?"

"I just know, that's all. Heaven is different from what anybody says. Sometimes I just know I'm going to get there early."

Hans looked at her in amazement. "What on earth are you talking about?"

"Heaven."

Hans remembered once when Lenchen was talking about heaven and angels to Father. "My dear child," Father said, "if only adults could hold fast to this faith."

Her answer stayed in Hans' memory. "Why, Father," Lenchen had said, "don't you believe it?"

"It took your father years to find faith," Aunt Lena said one time.

"Faith? What does that mean?" Hans asked.

"To believe God's promises are true," Aunt Lena answered.

Hans thought about faith and the invisible enemy to faith. He smiled, remembering the faith his two little brothers showed in their talking. "There'll be streams made of milk and white rolls will grow on every tree," little Martin told his younger brother Paul. "When we're in heaven, that's what we'll eat."

Lenchen explained her belief to Hans. "It's like Father said once. If he offered to give you a hundred gold coins which he had hidden under the table, and you said they were only lead, it would be your fault that you don't believe. Gold is gold, even if you don't think so. God doesn't lie when He promises eternal life. Our unbelief doesn't make God's promise empty."

How could Lenchen know and understand so much? Hans battled with secret fears about growing up, about not being the person others expected him to be. Lenchen, on the other hand, as good as said she expected to die young and was perfectly calm about the idea.

"Maybe I'm like that sow Father talked about," Hans thought. He couldn't help smiling about it.

"A sow lies on the manure as if on the finest

feather bed," Father had said, referring to people who are content not to become Christians. "She rests safely, snores tenderly, and sleeps sweetly. She does not fear king nor master, death nor hell, the devil nor God's wrath. She lives completely without worry."

Sometimes Father seemed to live without worry, too, when Mother showed him newly hatched chickens, or brought fruit from the orchard and flowers from the garden.

"Are all these things from our garden?" Father showed such disbelief that the Black Cloister gardens could produce such delights that the children laughed.

Father joked about Witten-berg, which means White Hill, because it was built on a sand belt.

"Little land, little land,
You are but a heap of sand.
If I dig you, the soil is light.
If I reap you, the yield is slight."

"But Doctor, that isn't true," Mother replied with spirit.

Father teased her. "Think of all the squabbles Adam and Eve must have had. Eve would say, 'You ate the apple,' and Adam would retort, 'You gave it to me.'"

But Father looked forward to the pears, grapes, and apples in the autumn as much as the children did.

"Oh, that we might look forward to judgment day in such joyful expectation!" He laughed.

Why couldn't people always live like that, Hans wondered. He remembered Father saying that God worked by opposites. A man would feel himself to be lost at the very moment when he was on the point of being saved.

Hans tried to figure out the puzzle. Maybe for people seeking faith, the invisible enemy was really a friend. Anyway, as Father said, people should not question why God allowed certain things. Mother had said once, "'If it were in my hands, I would really try to get even with my enemies. Why does God spare them so?"

"If God were to do everything with His strength," Father answered, "where would that leave His wisdom and His goodness? He overlooks many things so that His wisdom and goodness may become known in our weakness."

Hans was satisfied — for the time being.

A TEACHER OF PREACHERS

THE NEXT spring Hans and Lenchen watched visitors stream into the Black Cloister. Father, Philip Melanchthon, Justus Jonas, and John Bugenhagen were waiting to discuss church business with the visitors.

Two of the guests stood near Hans and Lenchen and chatted. Hans resented the critical tone of one man.

"So this is Wittenberg! It's my first visit here. Such old, ugly, squat wooden houses — more like a village than a town."

"It will be remembered as long as Martin Luther's name is," the other laughed.

"That may be true," the first man went on, "but Wittenberg is not worthy of being called a town. Unhealthy, disagreeable climate. All the roads, paths, and alleys are filled with rotting garbage, and the marketplace is a heap of stinking animal manure."

"But we have many bakers, shoemakers, tailors, clothmakers, and wagoners here. Besides Wittenberg supplies the whole region with salt," the second man said cheerfully.

The first man grunted. "Be that as it may, I'm here to see for myself what the so-called great man has to say."

Hans exchanged glances with Lenchen. What right did a visitor have to be so critical? No one forced him to come.

"Which one is Dr. Luther?" the first man asked.

"That round-faced man with a dimple in his chin."

"You mean the plump one who looks as if he's leaning backward?"

"Yes. I remember him as a monk. He was thin then, with furrows in his cheeks, but he had the same stubborn chin and glittering eyes."

Hans always looked at Father in a new light when people talked about him. The Martin Luther they saw was not the father he knew — or was he? Father laughed, joked, made up funny poems, lost his temper, apologized, studied, prayed, preached, wrote, and wrestled with the devil, whom he blamed for his illnesses.

"You don't know the meaning of hope until you've been tempted," Father always said. He had his own ways of dealing with the devil. "When I go to bed, the devil is always waiting for me," he would say. "I say, 'Devil, I must sleep. God commands, "Work by day. Sleep by night." So go away.' If that doesn't work and he brings out a catalog of sins, I say, 'Yes, old fellow, I know all about it. And I know some more you have overlooked.

Here are a few extra. Put them down.' If he still won't quit and presses me hard, I say, 'Saint Satan, pray for me. Of course you have never done anything wrong in your life. You alone are holy. Go to God and get grace for yourself. If you want to straighten me out, I say,"Physician, heal thyself." ' "

Father always said the devil could not stand mirth or music. Today everyone was laughing at Father's jokes. Only the critical guest near Hans and Lenchen kept on grumbling.

"Strange that a man like Luther could descend from a line of peasants," the critic was saying.

"Why do you say that? He married into nobility."

"Look at those hands. They're a peasant's hands."

Hans twitched with annoyance at the visitor's words. He wanted to say that Grandfather had worked his way up to become a manager of mines, but Hans knew he had to keep silent. It was only because Father had not noticed Lenchen and him that they were allowed to linger near the guests.

Other people talked among themselves.

"Dr. Luther doesn't know what he's thinking until he hears himself say it," Hans heard someone say.

Was that a compliment or a slur? Hans could not decide.

Another man complained to a companion, "Did you see that gold ring Dr. Luther wears? It bothers many people that he wears such a flashy gold ring. Of course it doesn't bother me, but it does upset some folks."

It amazed Hans that people who were supposed to be friends of Father criticized him like that.

Still another said, "They say his wife rules him."

"And he is glad of it," someone else retorted. "He is free to do his work."

Someone must have passed the remark on to Father. He laughed. "This reminds me of one of Aesop's fables," he said. "A lion invited all the animals to his evil-smelling cave. He asked the wolf how it smelled. 'It stinks,' the wolf replied. The donkey tried to flatter the lion: 'It smells good.' The fox said, 'I have a cold in my head.' Now, isn't that reply fitting? 'I have a cold in my head' means 'I am not at liberty to say anything.' "

Guests wandered over the courtyard, admiring the flowers and fruit trees. Father talked to first one, then another, answering their questions. Sometimes he was serious and sometimes he joked.

"Dr. Luther," one man exclaimed, "you have always loved God."

"Loved God? I hated Him," Father retorted. "But Dr. Staupitz found the solution." Father pointed to the pear tree in the garden. "It was right there under that tree. Staupitz told me to study for my doctor's degree, then preach and teach Bible at the university. I stammered out fifteen reasons why I couldn't. 'So much work would kill me,' I told him. 'Quite all right,' he said. 'God has plenty of work for clever men to do in heaven.' "

To another man he said, "I've preached here for twenty-four years. I've walked to church so often that it wouldn't be at all surprising if I had worn out my feet as well as my shoes on the pavement. He added, "I often dream that I'm called on to preach but I can't find my outline."

Hans could see that the guests had many questions to ask Father. One was worried about good works.

Father seemed irritated. "Anyone who says the gospel requires good works for salvation, I say flat and plain, he is a liar."

"Oh, I didn't mean —" the man stammered.

"Faith and grace alone, without works — these are enough," Father said firmly. "How I used to worry over the expression, 'the righteousness of God'! But when I learned that the righteousness of God is His mercy, I was cheered. Faith is not a human act, but the grace of God."

"I'm still not sure about faith."

"Do you believe in Jesus Christ?" Father asked.

"Yes, of course."

"Then believe that the just shall live through his faith. God says, 'Do and believe what I tell you and leave the rest to Me.'"

When the man said Christ seemed far away, Father replied, "Christ is everywhere. We must turn our eyes away from ourselves. The Lord God, the Creator, is beyond space and time and ourselves."

Another man said he had heard that Christians who followed Father's teachings could do as they pleased. All they had to do was believe.

"My dear fellow, you must first be reborn," Father exclaimed. "Believe in God. He will make you into a new person with new desires. Then you can do what you want, because you will want to do what is right."

By this time all the guests had arrived and

Father invited them to the lecture hall. On the way, Martin and Paul on their wooden horses bumped into one of the men. It was by accident, Hans could see.

Aunt Lena hurried the boys out of the way. "Why did you do that?"

"God made me do it," Martin replied. "I'm angry with Him."

Father overheard and burst out laughing. "Never be angry with God, because He isn't angry with you." He mused, "I remember when Staupitz told me the very same thing because I was confessing everything, making everything a sin. We shouldn't annoy our Lord God with little sins."

Hans thought about his own little sins — daydreaming instead of studying when his tutor dozed, teasing his younger brothers, lacking self-control when his older cousins teased him, and not speaking up when people asked what he was going to do when he grew up. Everyone must have little sins, he decided. Father, too, with his quick anger. But Father didn't let that stop him. He kept right on praying and helping people, but sometimes what he wrote or preached made others uncomfortable.

Hans coaxed Lenchen to slip into the rear of the lecture hall with him and listen to the talk. The critical man they had heard before stood up in front of the group and asked Father a question.

"Why do you write so harshly, Dr. Luther?"

"Because my opponents are so stupid," Father retorted.

Hans nudged Lenchen. "See?"

Lenchen put a finger to her lips.

Father paced in front of the table. "Our Lord God sends thunder before a heavy shower," he explained, "and then lets it rain to soak the ground. I'm the thunder. Or, to explain it another way, I can cut through a willow branch with a bread knife, but to cut through tough oak requires an axe and wedge. Even with these, one can hardly split the oak."

A man in front of Hans stood up. "I've heard some people complain that you are not sufficiently Lutheran."

A ripple of laughter spread over the room.

"They say you incline toward the old church," the man went on.

Father smiled. "Twenty years ago, if anybody had told me I could no longer say mass, he would have had a fight on his hands. At that time I adored it with my whole heart. Heavens! what I went through before I summoned up courage to defy the laws of the church. No one need worry that I will ever return to those ways again."

The men leaned forward to hear what Father would say next.

"There are times when I think the last day is not far off. Great efforts are being made to advance the gospel, but it's like a candle. Just before it burns out, it makes a last great spurt, as if it would continue to burn for a long time, and then it goes out. Now it appears as if the gospel is going to spread far and wide, but I'm afraid that it could be extinguished in a jiffy and that the Day of Judgment will follow."

"But we are just getting started," someone protested.

Father seemed to regret his gloomy prediction. "God's plans are secret. We'll find out what they are when they happen — not before. 'Let not your hearts be troubled.' The Bible tells us to rejoice." Father smiled and added, "I preach this, but I haven't learned it yet myself."

The guest preachers chuckled.

"I preach to others but I don't follow my own advice."

Several men laughed out loud.

"But we learn as we're tempted. Christ says we should be glad. God is gracious. He won't take you by the throat. A Christian must be a cheerful person. If he isn't, the devil is tempting him."

When the questions turned more to church matters, Philip Melanchthon, second to Father as a reformer, spoke. He was small, frail, and gentle. He walked with a slight hitch in one shoulder and spoke with a lisp. Father had always told him, "You will take my place; your gifts are greater than mine and more blessed of God." Someone who knew that Father liked the Apostle Paul once asked what Paul must have looked like. "A scrawny shrimp like Melanchthon," Father joked.

Melanchthon once said he was married to scholarship. A visitor found him rocking a cradle with one hand and holding a book in the other. Father often teased him about astrology. "It's nothing but blind dice-throwing," Father said. When Melanchthon wanted to cast Father's horoscope, Father said he would have nothing to do with the "scabby art." He could not understand why the leading Greek scholar of his day would stoop to such a hobby. "Don't try to make me into a fixed star," he joked. "I am an irregular planet."

Father always said Melanchthon let others take advantage of him because he loved them and wanted to be of service to everybody. "But," Father said, "I tear into everybody and spare no one. God works through both of us." He thought Melanchthon used bad judgment in dedicating his books to Archbishop Albrecht of Mainz and King Henry VIII of England, in the hope of winning them over. "I think my way is still the best," Father stated. "I speak right out and scold my opponents like school-boys. A knotty stump requires a tough wedge."

In his talk today, Melanchthon explained, "The Word of God doesn't fall into empty space but spreads from here into every land."

These words stirred everyone's enthusiasm. There was a buzz of conversation through the lecture hall. Hans and Lenchen slipped out as quietly as they had entered. Outside in the hall they found Lippus and Jost, as well as Martin and Paul.

"What are they doing in there?" Martin asked.

"Just talking."

"Is that what grown-ups do?"

"Well, they write things," Hans said.

"And they teach," Lippus said.

"And preach," Jost added.

"But that's just talking. I want to do something when I grow up," Martin stated.

So Martin was feeling it, too. Boys had to do something or be someone, and they had to think about it early. Of course he was already enrolled in Wittenberg University, along with Lippus and Jost. Hans' name had been entered the day after his birth in 1533. He knew it was an honor given to the sons of professors and important citizens.

Little Paul spoke up. "I know what I'm going to do when I'm big. I'll be a doctor."

"Like Father?" Lenchen asked.

"No. Like Mother. I'll put bandages on people and feed them medicine from a big spoon."

"I want to work at the university," Lippus said.

"I want to fight for some cause," Jost announced.

Hans wasn't sure what he wanted to do. He wouldn't be reforming the church. Of that he was sure.

CHURCH BUSINESS

HANS HEARD visitors ask Father many questions about the new church.

"Just what is our church?" someone blurted.

"Every child of seven among us knows, thank God, what the dear term 'church' means," Father retorted. "It means the holy believers and the sheep who hear the Shepherd's voice." He went on. "Some say we can't build a new church. They think that would require thinking up new ceremonies. They don't realize that building up the church means to lead consciences from doubt and murmuring to faith, knowledge, and certainty."

Another mentioned the many martyrs who died for their faith. "Why does God permit this?" he asked.

Father had a prompt answer. "God didn't hinder Pharaoh's ungodly plans. 'Why' is not for us to ask. God says, 'Why I do what I do is not for you to know, but believe in Christ, pray, and I will make everything turn out well.' "

A man ventured a joke. "Maybe there wouldn't be so much trouble now if you hadn't wanted to do away with the pope."

"I never said that," Father snapped. "It is possible to live with the unnecessary laws of the pope, monasteries, religious foundations, princes, and rulers. A free Christian can do this, not to get to heaven, but to set an example to the pope, the bishop, and the community." Father's voice rose. Hans could see Father's quick anger coming to the surface.

Father went on. "Although tyrants do wrong in making such demands, they do me no harm, provided they are not against God. The pope's authority does not reach as far as the soul. The soul is free." By this time Father's voice was like thunder.

Afterward, he admitted, "My temper gets me in trouble sometimes, but for the most part my anger is necessary and just. I have other sins that are greater."

Hans thought about what Father had said. Father's anger, like a thunderstorm, always cleared the air.

Father showed irritation later when a newcomer to the Black Cloister knelt in front of him. "O blessed Martin Luther, you have given me the Bible."

"Up, up, my good man," Father snorted. "You are kneeling like a Catholic before a shrine."

Another guest murmured in an aside, "I don't think a great leader of the church should lose his temper like that."

A man defended Father. To Hans' amazement,

88

the word "thunderstorm" came up in the very way he himself had thought of it.

"Dr. Luther can't be blamed for what he says any more than you blame a thunderstorm which clears the air and brings the rain that allows crops to grow," the man said. "If it tears down a fence or lights a straw roof on fire, can you blame the storm?"

Thunder had really played a large part in Father's life, Hans reflected. Father often used the term in answering questions. When someone asked about free will, Father exclaimed, "God accomplishes all things by His eternal law. By this thunderbolt free will sinks shattered in the dust. Mankind has a free will, but it is to milk cows, build houses, and so on, but no further."

When someone mentioned heretics, Father recalled Sylvester Prierias, who censored books and looked for heretics. "Whoever questions a word or act of the Roman church is a heretic," Prierias had thundered.

"At that time I was still weak," Father said. "I didn't want to attack the church. I had respect for such arguments."

Many asked questions about organizing the new church.

"It is impossible to set everything going at once," Father declared. "All we have done is to sow the seed. If it comes up, there may be so many weeds that we will be kept busy pulling them up."

For Father, church business always came back to preaching the faith. "I will preach the Word, I will speak it, I will write it, but I will not force anyone.

Faith must be free, not forced."

"What about preaching?" a man asked. "How do you know if you're called?"

Father had a ready answer. "No good work is undertaken or done with careful thought," Father stated with conviction. "It must all happen in a half-sleep. This is how I was forced to take up the office of preaching. If I had known what I know now, ten horses wouldn't have driven me to it."

Everyone gasped.

"Unless a preacher finds joy in his work, he will have trouble," Father continued. "Our Lord God had to ask Moses six times to be His spokesman in Egypt. He led me into the office in the same way. Had I known beforehand. He would have had to take more pains to get me in. I would not take the whole world to enter upon this work now. On the other hand, I would not take the whole world not to have begun it."

Several of the listeners laughed. Others murmured agreement.

"If I were to write about the burdens of the preacher as I have experienced them and as I know them, I would scare everybody off." Father was warming up to his subject. "I wish nobody would be chosen preacher unless he had first taught school. Now all the young fellows want to start out as preachers and flee from schoolwork. But if he has taught school for one to ten years, he can leave with a good conscience. Teaching involves much work and yet it does not bring one much honor. If I weren't a preacher, I know no position on earth I'd rather fill than that of schoolmaster."

Father explained that a preacher is like a carpenter, and his tool the Word of God. "The materials on which he works vary. He builds various things in various ways. Sometimes he consoles, sometimes frightens; sometimes he scolds, or sometimes soothes."

A visiting minister confessed that preaching was a burden to him. "My sermons are too short."

"If Peter and Paul were here, they would scold you because you wish right off to be as accomplished as they," Father answered. "Crawling is something, even if one is unable to walk. Do your best. If you cannot preach an hour, preach half an hour or a quarter of an hour. Don't try to imitate other people. Center on the heart of the matter and leave the rest to God."

"But Dr. Luther, you have it easy. You've had so much practice."

Father grunted. "Every time I have to preach, I'm afraid. You'll find out three things, just as I have. First, you've prepared the best you can, and the sermon will slip through your fingers like water. Next, you may abandon your outline and God will give you grace. Third, you won't have been able to pull anything together, and you will preach acceptably. So leave it to God."

A young man asked, "Teach me in a brief way how to preach."

"First you must learn to go up to the pulpit," Father joked.

Everyone laughed. Hans wondered why. Was it because all the pulpits were raised above the congregation and the preacher had to climb a little stairs to get to it?

Father did not explain, but went right on. "Second, you must stay there for a time. Third, you must learn how to get down again."

The young man scowled and bit his lip. After a discussion his face cleared. What Father was really saying seemed to make sense to the young man. First, he should have a divine call, second, a pure doctrine, and third, not preach more than an hour.

Father joked about preachers who preached long sermons on whatever came to mind. "They remind me of the way women usually talk," Father said. "It's like a maidservant on her way to market. When she meets another maid she stops to chat with her for a while. Then she meets another maid and talks with her, and so on. She gets to market very slowly."

Hans knew Father meant Pomeranus. Mother herself had remarked more than once that Pomeranus wandered too far from his subject when he preached.

Father thought Wenceslaus Link, who succeeded John von Staupitz as vicar-general of the Augustinians, was the best preacher. "He teaches in a plain, childlike, popular, and simple way. I prefer to preach in an easy and comprehensible fashion, too, but when it comes to arguments at the university, there I'll make it sharp enough for anybody."

Father advised preaching to the common people. "It's to them I preach, for they need to understand. If the others, masters and doctors, don't want to listen, they can leave. Be simple and direct. Be a preacher to unschooled youth, to sixteen-year-old girls, women, old men, and farmers. They don't understand lofty matters. Christ could have taught in a profound way, but He delivered His message with the utmost simplicity so that the common people could understand. He spoke about sheep, shepherds, wolves, vineyards, fig trees, seeds, fields, plowing. Lay people were able to understand these things."

"How can you tell when you're ready to look for a pulpit?" someone asked.

"Offer your services when a position is unoccupied," Father advised. "Don't force your way in, but indicate you are prepared. It is like a girl who is trained for marriage. If the right person asks her, she gets married. To force one's way in is to push somebody else out, but to offer one's service is to say, 'I'll be glad to accept if you can use me in this place.' So Isaiah said, 'Here I am. Send me.'" He went when he heard that a preacher was needed.

Father warned would-be preachers to remain humble. "People think they can know everything by simply listening to a sermon. I don't even understand the full meaning yet of 'Our Father who art in heaven.' ""

This remark brought a discussion of Father's translation of the Bible.

"It all started from my early work in the mud," Father said. "I knew the common people needed to have the Bible in their own language. I worked all alone for ten years in preparing it."

A student reminded the group that there were already translations of the Bible in German.

93

"Yes, but they were awkward," another student said. "For example, in one German Bible part of Psalm 23 reads: 'Your rod and your staff, the same have comforted me.' Another reads, 'Your rod and your crutch,' and still another, 'Your broom and your cudgel.'"

Father laughed. "I put it, 'Your rod and staff comfort me.'"

"Here's another example," the student said. "In Psalm 50 one German Bible says, 'Call on me in the day of tribulation, and I redeem you, and you honor me.'" Then he quoted Father's translation: "'Call upon me in trouble, and I will save you, and you will praise me.'"

"To think that some people still criticize the new Bible!" someone exclaimed.

"Yes," Father said, "now that it is put into German and finished, anyone can read and master it. Anyone can now run his eye over three or four pages without stumbling once. He will not be aware of the rocks and boulders, because he will now pass over them as over a well-planed board. It is easy to plow a field that has been cleared. But no one wants to uproot the forest and tree trunks and put the field in order."

Father sighed, as if remembering. "Sometimes my qualifications to translate the Scriptures have been questioned. You are doctors? I ask. So am I. You are theologians? So am I. You write books? So do I. I can translate. You cannot do this."

Father explained how he had read the Bible again and again. "Only then did I consult writers of books about the Bible, but I had to wrestle with the Bible

94

itself. It's better to see with one's own eyes than with another's." In an aside, he said, "I wish that all my books were buried. Otherwise, everybody will imitate me and try to become famous by writing."

It was a tremendous job to make the Hebrew writers talk German. They were stubborn. They did not like to give up their Hebrew and follow the barbaric German tongue. It was like asking a nightingale to forsake her lovely melody and imitate the monotonous call of the cuckoo. Father explained how he listened to mothers in their homes, the children in the streets, the common man in the marketplace to see how they spoke. He translated accordingly.

"It took about ten weeks to translate the New Testament," he said. He was in Wartburg Castle at the time. Later, he improved it with the help of Philip Melanchthon. "I had choked over the Bible. All previous interpretations had failed to speak to me." He translated from the original Greek, later from Reuchlin's Hebrew grammar, and from the Greek New Testament published by Erasmus.

The next time Hans had to read from the Bible at breakfast he wondered what it would be like to be a translator. His tutor, Herr Weller, suggested that Hans translate from German to Latin. Hans struggled all day on one passage. When he handed it to his tutor, Herr Weller read it and burst into laughter. Hans felt crushed. What kind of knowledge did Father have that he could translate the whole New Testament in ten weeks? Hans brooded over his lack of understanding. Even Lenchen could not cheer him up. Mother worried. Aunt Lena worried.

"It's too noisy here," Mother told Aunt Lena.

"But he has a good tutor," Hans heard Aunt Lena reply.

"Perhaps the younger children are too bothersome," Mother continued, "and the older cousins tease him too much."

Hans did not know himself what was the matter. He felt as if a stone rested on his chest.

Father worried, too. "We'll send him away to school," he decided.

When Hans heard about the decision, he felt worse than ever. Leave Mother, Aunt Lena, and Lenchen? Even his bothersome young brothers, Martin and Paul? He dreaded the thought.

Father's Strassburg friend Wolfgang Capito wrote on July 20, 1536, and asked that Hans be entrusted to him and his friends. They would do their best for Hans.

"Strassburg is too far away," Mother said, and Father agreed.

Another friend, Comerarius, lived in Tübingen, but it too was farther away than Mother and Father wanted to consider.

"I don't have to go," Hans told Lenchen in triumph later. "I'll try harder right here."

He still worried inwardly. He was Martin Luther's son. How could he ever compete with his famous father?

DEEP TROUBLE

THE THOUGHT of being sent away to school haunted Hans.

"But boys are supposed to go away," Lenchen told him. "Father did. He even went piggyback." She giggled and added, "Ask Aunt Lena."

Aunt Lena explained that when Father was five, an older relative carried him piggyback to school in Mansfeld. "It was too far to walk," she said.

Hans learned that Father had gone to school there for eight years. He called the teachers tyrants and jailers. The teacher sat at a high desk with a birch switch the size of a garden broom. Once Father had been birched fifteen times in one morning because he did not know his Latin grammar lesson, but he had not been taught how to do it. There were so many students of different ages in the room, Father had been overlooked.

When Father went to school, if any student used a German word instead of Latin, a classroom spy would shout, "Wolf!" A wooden donkey's halter was hung around the offender's neck for punishment.

Hans shuddered. He would hate to have a donkey halter around his neck here at the Black Cloister, but he had to admit he gave his tutor, Herr Weller, cause enough.

Aunt Lena mused aloud. "Sometimes I think your father's early school experience led him to use German in the church. At any rate," she went on, "when he went to Eisenach and attended the parish school of St. George, he liked it very much, and always speaks of his 'dear Eisenach.' "

Hans found out that before Father went to Eisenach, he had gone to Latin School in Magdeburg, run by the Brethren of the Common Life.

"How old was he?" Hans asked.

"Fourteen."

Older than I am now, Hans reflected, and felt a surge of hope. Maybe he wouldn't be sent away just yet. But he knew Mother and Father were still talking about it. If only he could do better in Latin and music — the very things Father was so good at!

At bedtime, Aunt Lena told the children about Father's schooldays. In Eisenach, Father played the lute and in the customary way, he and other schoolboys went from door to door to earn food with their songs. "They were called 'crumb-seekers,' " Aunt Lena explained.

"I wish we could do that," little Martin said. He was always ready for any action.

"We can't go around *begging*," Lenchen told him. "People would think Father wasn't taking care of his family."

"But we're poor, aren't we, Aunt Lena?" Martin asked.

She smiled. "Some people might think so."

"Mother is always worrying about how she's going to feed so many people."

"And God always provides, just the way Father says," Lenchen assured him. "We have a vegetable garden, fruit trees, fishponds, and cows. People send gifts all the time."

Hans agreed, but he continued to worry about being the son of a famous father. If only Grandfather had remained a peasant instead of becoming the manager of a mine! Father had always said he thought God had never given more than He gave to the peasants — cheese, eggs, butter, oats, barley, apples, and pears. Hans smiled remembering once when he was little Father had asked him, "How much do you think you cost me yearly?" Hans had said, "Father, you don't buy food and drink, but apples and pears cost a lot of money." Father had smiled and said it was the other way around. Later, Father talked about foolish grown-ups who thought nothing of what God gave them to keep them alive, but valued highly things without worth.

Sometimes Hans heard houseguests talk about Father's background.

"Dr. Luther's father couldn't be a peasant. He mined copper."

"But you've heard him yourself say, 'I am from a peasant family. My father, my grandfather, my forebears were true peasants,'" another retorted.

"Well, then, his mother wasn't a peasant."

"Yes, she was. Dr. Luther said himself that she

carried wood on her back from the forest."

"But everyone did that. It was the custom."

It was according to custom, too, Hans learned, that the youngest in a family inherited the homestead. Grandfather was the oldest of four sons, and he had to leave and make his living elsewhere. When he married, he and Grandmother settled first at Eisleben, where Father was born.

By questioning Aunt Lena and listening to people talk, Hans learned about Father's boyhood in bits and pieces. Mining people where Grandfather and Grandmother lived believed in spirits, demons, and devils. Grandmother was sure that the death of one of her children was caused by a neighbor who was a witch.

Hans heard Father tell a houseguest, "My father once whipped me so severely that I ran away, and he was worried that he might not win me back again. I wouldn't beat my children, lest they should become shy and hate me. I know nothing that would give me greater sorrow."

Father explained that his parents wanted the best for him but treated him more roughly than they should have. Grandmother had once beaten Father until he bled over a single stolen nut. "Too much strictness makes a child numb," Father said. "When you punish, see that there is an apple by the stick."

Many guests were curious about the religious training of children at the Black Cloister.

"Though I am a learned doctor," Father said, "I haven't yet progressed beyond teaching my children the Ten Commandments, the Creed, and the Lord's

Prayer. I still go over these every day with my children."

He explained the Sunday devotional hour. The whole family, including students and hired help, gathered for worship. One of Father's helpers, Veit Dietrich, took notes on Father's talks. Every child who could read took turns in reading from the Bible after the prayer and before meals.

Visitors often inquired what the children would be when they grew up. Hans still cringed every time someone asked about that. It brought up the same questions that had bothered him for a long time. Each time he tried to compare himself to Father. How could he compete? What could he ever do that would amount to anything?

"Did you know that Grandfather wanted Father to be a lawyer?" Lenchen asked Hans one day. "He was very angry when Father became a monk."

Hans marveled at the strange ways of parents and children. He himself secretly wanted to study law, maybe not to be a lawyer, but to know some of the mysteries about law that always made Father so angry whenever he had to deal with lawyers. Father didn't even want to make a will. He said God would provide. How angry he had been about the inheritance from Grandfather of twelve hundred and fifty gulden divided into five parts. His own relatives wanted his share. "If they act this way when I'm alive," Father had said, "what will they do to my children when I die?" Then he added, "We will have a richer reward with God than my relatives who are as poor as beggars before Him."

Whenever Father talked about God's rewards or

gifts, Hans started worrying again. "God hasn't bestowed any gifts on *me*," he told himself. Even worse, Father used to worry in the same way.

"I remember Pomeranus would scold me," Father told a visitor. "He'd ask me what I meant when I said I was the victim of God's wrath. 'What am I to do with this man,' God said. 'I have bestowed so many excellent gifts on him, and yet he doesn't trust me for his salvation?' That sounded like the voice of an angel to me."

At least Father hadn't started his life's work when he was as young as I am, Hans reflected. He asked Aunt Lena, "When did Father know he was going to start a new church and translate the Bible?"

"He didn't know," Aunt Lena explained patiently. "You see, you have to prepare for your lifework ahead of time, even though you don't know what the outcome will be." She laughed. "For example, fifteen years ago I hadn't the slightest idea I'd be here in the Black Cloister taking care of you children. I planned to spend my whole life in the convent."

Hans grinned, remembering the story of how Father had once teased Aunt Lena by saying all escaped nuns were going to be put back in their convents. When he asked her if she wanted to go, she was so shaken she blurted out "No" in Latin instead of German.

Hans still had questions to ask. "Did Father know he was going to become famous?"

"Do you know what you are going to be?" Aunt Lena countered.

102

"No, but that's different." *I'm not anything,*
Hans told himself. He went on. "You mean Father
had no idea that he was going to be a reformer?"

"How could he? God doesn't call people until
they are prepared. They have to receive their education first."

Hans tried to understand. It was all very well to
study first, like Father, learning Latin, Greek,
and Hebrew. *But for what lifework should I be preparing myself?*

It was a relief to play with his younger brothers.
Hans envied their carefree life.

"Let's play *Wartburg Castle,*" little Martin
shouted. "Hans, you can be Father." He and Paul
raced around getting ready.

Hans agreed gloomily. He let Martin jump from
the shrubbery and capture him, Bible and all. They
rode furiously on stick horses to the drawbridge,
then put a ladder up the wall for Hans to climb.
When Hans pulled the ladder up, Paul shouted,
"Now you can translate the Bible."

Hans winced. He could not forget how Herr
Weller had laughed at his translation of a short
passage. Hans did not want to play Father anymore, but he could not spoil his brothers' joy in
enacting Father's capture and imprisonment by
friends.

Later, Hans welcomed the chance to go to the
marketplace, and when he saw his old enemy,
Blacky, the peasant, Hans was glad. He had not
seen Blacky for a long time, and he had an old
score to settle with him.

At first Blacky did not see Hans. When he did,

he scowled and then grinned. Hans knew what Blacky was thinking. Today would be a showdown, once for all. The ditch with its sewage and rotting garbage smelled to the skies this hot day. One of the two was going to land in it.

Hans whooped out a battle cry. If he could just get his hands on Blacky, all the worries and depressions of the past weeks would be gone. A fight was just what he needed to clear the air, and Hans was out to win.

Blacky must have felt the same way. The two boys eyed each other warily and edged toward the ditch. Hans tensed, clenching and unclenching his fists. From the corner of his eye he saw something that made him hesitate. Lenchen and one of the maids from the Black Cloister had come to the marketplace, too. Still, he needn't worry about his sister. He could count on her to understand.

But the moment he had taken to think about Lenchen proved Hans' undoing. Blacky ran up, grabbed him by the waist, and threw Hans off balance. Before he could recover, Blacky simply waltzed him to the edge of the ditch, gave him a shove, and it was all over. Hans flailed his arms. The stinking muck splattered his face, matted his hair, and sloshed around him when he tried to get on his feet. Dimly, he heard Lenchen scream. The next moment there was another splash. Blacky landed beside him, flailed his arms like Hans, and emerged gasping.

Lenchen stood with her hands on her hips, glaring at Blacky. Hans realized she had pushed Blacky in. She took a step forward to help Hans, but the smell must have been too much. She hurried off.

The two boys stared at each other. Blacky was dabbing at his slimy clothes. Somehow, it struck Hans funny. In trying to climb out, Blacky slipped. Hans grabbed his hand and helped Blacky to the street. Then they both burst into laughter. They cleaned each other off as best they could.

"Let's go to the river," Hans suggested. He knew he could never go back to the Black Cloister with his clothes smelling this way.

"All right," Blacky agreed.

They tried to sneak past the town gate. The gatekeeper and a guard laughed at them.

"You boys out for a little swim?" one asked innocently.

"Did you ever think of trying the Wittenberg River?" the other joked.

Hans and Blacky ducked past them and headed for the Elbe River. They splashed in the water, clothes and all, until the last rotten smell was gone.

"You don't go to the marketplace often, do you?" Blacky asked on their way back. "I've been watching for you."

"You have? Well, I have to stay at home and study a lot."

"What do you study?"

"Latin, mostly."

"Do you have to be rich to learn Latin?"

Hans laughed. "We're not rich. You just have to study, that's all."

Blacky surprised Hans by asking, "Do you think someone like me could learn Latin?"

"Sure. I'll teach you, if you want to start."

"But I'm only a peasant."

"That doesn't matter — being a peasant, I mean. So was my grandfather, but he didn't stay a peasant. If you work, you can be educated by your church. That's what my father did."

Blacky came to the courtyard every day and gradually they forgot they had been enemies. Hans drilled him on Latin grammar. To Hans' surprise, he found that teaching Blacky helped him in his own study. Blacky worked hard to memorize all the Latin Hans shared with him. By the end of summer, Blacky had caught the attention of a priest. "I'm going to be educated for the church," he announced proudly one day. "I'm going to be a priest."

How fast things had happened! Now Blacky knew what he was going to do with his life, and Hans still didn't know. How would he ever find out?

A GROWING HOUSEHOLD

A VISITING preacher stopped Hans in the downstairs passageway after breakfast one morning.

"Well, well, son, so you're to be the great preacher of the gospel," he boomed in a hearty voice.

"Why, no, sir, not at all. Father says my little brother is to be a preacher." Hans ducked into the shadows but could not escape from the attention of the preacher.

"You are the oldest son of Martin Luther, aren't you?"

"Yes." Hans looked longingly at the sunny courtyard. Why did visitors have to be so inquisitive? And why did they always get things mixed up? Little Martin was to be the preacher, not Hans. If this preacher didn't stop talking, Hans would not have any time to play in the courtyard before going to his Latin lesson.

"You are to preach the gospel," the visitor insisted. "Your father said so at court, in the presence of Pietro Paolo Vergerio."

"Who is he?"

"Why, he's the representative Pope Paul sent here to Wittenberg last November. Your father really bragged about you, and how he has announced to the world that you are going to preach the gospel."

Hans cringed. How could he be like Father, who preached several times a week, and who often gathered the whole household together to try out a sermon on them? Father never ran out of something to say even though he sometimes joked about his sermons falling flat.

"But I can't talk that much," Hans blurted to the visitor. "I don't want to be a preacher." He excused himself and ran upstairs. When had Father made such a statement? Was it really last November?

"Don't you remember when Father and Dr. Pomeranus had breakfast at the castle last November?" Lenchen asked. With gleaming eyes, she described how Father had dressed up in a dark shirt with satin trimmed sleeves, a golden chain around his neck, several rings, and a serge coat trimmed with fox fur. "And he shaved extra carefully," she giggled, "because he wanted to look young. He told Mother that Rome would know he could accomplish many things — he wasn't worn out yet." She added, "He and Dr. Pomeranus rode in a coach to the castle, and Father called himself the German pope as a joke. Where were you? It isn't every day that Father dresses up."

Try as he would, Hans could not remember that November day. He was probably with his tutor, Herr Weller. As far as Father's dressing up was con-

cerned, what would people have thought if they saw
him, as Hans did a little later, mending his trousers
in the way he had learned as a monk?

"I have mended these three times," Father grum-
bled, "and I will mend them again before I have new
ones made. Tailors are careless. They use a lot of
material and don't give trousers the proper shape."
He threaded a needle and went on. "In Italy,
tailors who make nothing but trousers have their own
guild. In Germany, trousers, shirts, and coats are all
made from the same pattern."

Mother reminded him of the time he needed a
patch and cut one from little Hans' trousers. Everyone laughed, and Father laughed, too. Little Martin
pranced around the family room trying to balance a
spool of thread on his nose. Father asked him twice
for it, but Martin, who always had a mind of his
own, pretended not to hear.

"You are a little rogue." Father sighed. "I'm
worried about what will become of you. You act
like a little lawyer." Father's voice rose, as it always did when he talked about doctors of medicine
or lawyers. "No son of mine will ever enter a school
of law." He pointed his needle at Hans. "You will
be a theologian."

Hans ducked his head. He ought to protest.
Father would listen. He wanted the best for his
children, Hans knew. *But what can I say? I don't
even know what I want to do.* He was relieved when
Father started talking about the old days.

Once Father had walked from Wittenberg to
Cologne. "It took two months," Father declared.
Now Father traveled by horseback or carriage. "I

109

must have covered ten thousand miles by this time," he said. "Our Paul will travel a lot, too, when he grows up and fights the Turks." Father had often joked to visitors that he owed so much to the Apostle Paul he could have afforded to name two sons after him.

When Mother, always a worrier, heard the word "Turks," she shuddered and started talking in her usual rapid way about the ever-present threat of invasion. "God should wipe them out," she declared.

Although Father took the threat of invasion seriously, too, he teased Mother about her chatter. Father interrupted. "Dear Kathe, did you say the Lord's Prayer before beginning your sermon?" He had often told visitors at the supper table that women are talkers by nature, but men have to learn the art by great effort. "If only the meaning of women's long speeches were something other than 'Give me money,'" he said, and then added, "But women have a sharper weapon than their tongue — tears." Whenever he said that, he and Mother exchanged smiles.

Hans knew, like everyone else, that Father enjoyed family life, visitors, good talk, and the music that always brought him out of troubled moods. Whenever Father took fifteen minutes to tune his lute, Hans knew there would be a musical evening.

"Music soothes the soul," Father always said. "It is no invention of ours; it is the gift of God. I place it next to theology." Father had a beautiful singing voice as well as a keen ear. He could always tell when Hans was off-key, even in a group. *Why can't I be musical, like Martin, Paul, and even baby Margarete?* She bounced and gurgled in Mother's lap every time there was singing. Still, it was comforting to know that Lenchen wasn't musical, either, even though they both took part in the household singing.

Father had already written more than thirty hymns. Sometimes he put Latin hymns into German, or used psalms, or chants with familiar tunes. Hans' favorite was "A Mighty Fortress Is Our God." When the whole household burst out into this hymn, the walls almost bulged out. The town church choir and congregation sang it, too. Father had started the choir and congregational singing. He wanted to reach the young people, he said. The older ones could go their ways. "We must read, sing, preach, write, and compose verse," he said. "If it were possible, I would let all the bells peal, all the organs thunder, and everyone sing at the top of his voice," Father told visiting preachers. "Young people must constantly be exposed to music, for it produces good character. Music is the greatest gift of God. The devil simply cannot stand it," he always added. "It drives away many severe temptations."

Father liked three- and four-part music. "When natural music is sharpened and polished by art, one sees the great and perfect wisdom of God in creating us with the ability to sing. It is possible to sing a simple tune, while at the same time three, four, or five other voices play and leap around this simple tune as if in rejoicing."

Father had even joked about his struggles with Rome in terms of music. When he first broke with the church, he called it a prelude and said that he would break into another little song in a still higher key.

If anyone disapproved of the congregation singing, Father would say, "I am sure it is no secret to any Christian that it is a good thing and pleases God to sing spiritual songs. The prophets and kings in the Old Testament praised God by singing songs to the accompaniment of cymbals and stringed instruments. Psalm-singing has been known to the whole Christian church from the beginning."

"Why are Dr. Luther's words so powerful?" a visitor once asked.

"Because he knows music," someone retorted.

"Since the Lord our God has poured such noble gifts as music into this life," Father told a visitor, "what is it going to be like in heaven, where everything will be so completely perfect?"

No one could answer that question, not even Lenchen, who smiled a secret smile as if she knew more than she could tell about a future perfect life.

But music did not prevent Father from having problems in his growing household. Hans Polner, a son of Father's sister, had lived at the Black Cloister for some time. He had a terrible temper and would fly into rages. Then he would get drunk.

"People like you should avoid wine like poison," Father raged in his turn. "Don't you ever think what shame you are bringing on yourself, on our house, on the city, and on the church?"

Hans found his cousin slumped in a dark corner one day. Was he drunk or thinking about something?

"Why do you drink so much, Cousin Hans?"

"I'm not drinking now," his cousin snapped. "It's just that I know what I have to do, and I don't want to do it yet."

Hans felt a sudden sympathy for his cousin. Was Hans Polner worried about what he was going to do with his life?

"What is it you have to do?" Hans asked.

His cousin stared gloomily ahead. "Well, I suppose I might as well tell you, because you have to be one, too."

"You mean you have to be a preacher? Did Father tell you?"

"No, he didn't tell me. That's the whole trouble. I'm telling myself — or something inside me is telling me. I guess it's God. But I don't want to — I don't want to, yet."

Hans remembered Father telling about the inner struggles he had had in the monastery. When Father felt an inward call, he had cried out, "Not me! Not me!" Did that mean Father hadn't wanted to do what he was called upon by God to do?

Hans took a deep breath. A kind of dim understanding was coming to him. His cousin was going through an interior struggle too. Why didn't he just give in and say he was going to be a preacher?

To Hans' surprise, his cousin struggled to his feet. "I might as well face it," he said with a wry grin. "I'm going to be a preacher someday. How about you?"

"Oh, no, I couldn't," Hans exclaimed.

"Well, you're young yet. You wait. Someday you'll have to give in, too."

But day after day Hans Luther still worried about

113

his own future. If he could just say to himself, "Yes, I'm going to be a preacher." Father had said so. *Why can't I say it?*

Aunt Lena laughed sympathetically when he told her about it. "You must remember that your father had the same problem with *his* father. Your grandfather wanted your father to be a lawyer."

In a flash, Hans understood something. Father had resisted Grandfather because God had wanted Father to do something else.

"Your grandfather was very angry when your father became a monk," Aunt Lena continued, "but two of your uncles died from the plague, and your grandfather was not so insistent after that."

Hans learned that Father's closest friend had been killed in a fight at Erfurt University, and once Father had almost bled to death when he had accidentally cut an artery with his own sword.

"But you must leave these things to God," Aunt Lena said. "When the right time comes, you will know what you are to do. You will have no hesitation and no doubt." She smiled. "If you worry, it is as your father says, just beating your fists at the air."

Hans tried to forget about his own problem and think about other things that were going on in the Luther household. Some were amusing, like Cousin Fabian's afternoon naps in the barn, and the time he almost lay on a nest of snakes. There were the girls to worry about — Lena Kaufmann, Else Kaufmann, and Anna Strauss. Lena Kaufmann had fallen in love with father's helper, Veit Dietrich, but Father did not approve of marrying so young.

"I know that you would take good care of my niece," he had told Veit Dietrich, "but I don't know if she would take good care of you. She has to grow up more, and if she doesn't want to mind me, then I will give her to a worthless hired man and not cheat a good fellow like you." He explained that it was not wise for young people to marry quickly. "If they do, the little dog, Regret, may come along and bite them."

Hans thought too much fuss was being made over his girl cousins. Why were they so eager to marry?

"Because they see how happy Mother and Father are," Lenchen said.

She had a point, Hans admitted. Just the same, he was glad he didn't have to worry about marriage. He had problems enough figuring out who he was.

TABLE TALK

BEFORE supper, Father gathered the children into the family room for a story, one of Aesop's fables. Next to the Bible, Father thought Aesop was the best moral teacher.

"The wolf said to the lamb, 'You have muddied the water for me,'" Father began. "The lamb said, 'Not at all. You are below me in the brook.' That is how the lamb excused himself, by referring to the circumstances. Then the wolf said, 'You have nibbled off my meadow near the woods.' The lamb said, 'But I have no teeth, for I am still young.' In this way he excused himself again. The wolf said, 'Your father did this to me.' The lamb said, 'What does that have to do with me?' Then the wolf said, 'No matter how smart you try to be in excusing yourself, I'm going to eat you up anyhow.'"

Little Martin and Paul played wolf and lamb until supper was ready. Hans puzzled over the lesson the story was meant to give. Was it that no

Before supper, Father gathered the children into the family room to tell them one of Aesop's fables.

matter how he argued with himself, life was going to eat him up? He shook off the thought and went to the washroom with the others. Father washed his hands and became thoughtful as he often did about simple household matters.

"How dirty the water gets! We must not forget that our skin and flesh are made of dirt. It is as the Scripture says, "We are dust and ashes."

Students, guests, and family gathered for the evening meal. As usual, several students had notebooks by their places to take notes on what Father said. His table talks had been famous for years. Students had even sold their notes on Father's talks.

Hans could see Mother trying to hide her annoyance. "They ought to pay for these extra lessons," she often said.

Everyone waited for Father to speak. Sometimes he ate in silence, as if he were still a monk, and then the students' notebooks remained blank.

"Well, gentlemen, what is the news?" Father asked.

Hans heard sighs of relief. Father would be talking tonight. Before the others had a chance to speak, Father mentioned his recent trip to Torgau, a few days' ride from Wittenberg. Torgau! The name struck a chill in Hans. He had overheard Father and Mother talk of sending him there to study before the year was out.

The students talked of the beginning of the new semester at Wittenberg University. Philip Melanchthon spoke of the high cost of living in Wittenberg. A student needed twice the money now as it had taken to meet his needs ten years ago.

Father agreed. "Yes, then one could buy fifteen eggs for four pieces of copper and a bushel of rye for two pieces of silver. A student could manage. Now everything sells for three times as much. Truly, the farmer has now learned arithmetic. He has learned how to double his prices."

Hans was not surprised when Father started to talk about God. Father always connected details of living with his beliefs.

"The best argument that there is a God, and it moves me deeply, is that a cow always bears a cow; a horse always bears a horse. No cow gives birth to a horse; no horse gives birth to a cow. Therefore, it is necessary to conclude that something directs everything in this way."

"Doctor," a student said, "I understand you know the Bible by heart."

Father laughed. "The Scriptures are a vast forest, but there's no tree in it that I haven't shaken with my hand. The monks gave me a Bible bound in red leather. I knew what was on every page. Sometimes one statement occupied all my thoughts for a whole day. For some years now I have read through the Bible twice a year. If you picture the Bible to be a mighty tree and every word a little branch, I have shaken every one of these branches because I wanted to know what it was and what it meant."

Sometimes at supper there was more talking than eating. "Wouldn't it be better to eat instead of talking so much?" Mother would murmur.

A guest once noted that Father ate a great deal.

Father overheard and smiled. "If our Lord creates nice, large fish in Kathe's pond, don't you think He expects me to eat them?"

He asked for more food, and when a servant did not bring it fast enough, his voice rose.

"Be patient," Mother said. "I'll get it for you. The servant is new."

Partly exasperated and partly amused, Father burst out, "I must be patient with the pope, I must be patient with the fanatics, I must be patient with the servants, I must be patient with Katherina von Bora, and my patience is so great that my whole life is nothing but patience." Then he smiled sheepishly and squeezed Mother's hand.

Another time he threw his hands up and told Mother, "Do what you please. You have complete control of the household, provided my rights are preserved." Then he teased her. "Female government has never done any good. God made Adam master over all creatures, to rule over all living things, but when Eve persuaded him that he was lord even over God, she spoiled everything. We have you women to thank for that!"

Mother raised her eyebrows and smiled.

Father smiled back. "It is the pleasantest kind of life to have a modest household, to live with an obedient wife, and to be content with little. I don't worry about debts, because as soon as they're paid, I know there'll be more," Father joked.

One evening licentiate Nicholas Amsdorf, lawyer Christopher Blank, Philip Melanchthon, and Dr. Melchior Kling, a member of the law faculty at Wittenberg University, were guests at the Black Cloister.

Father complained about how poor preachers were. "They're opposed on every hand, especially by noblemen who watch them with sharp eyes and rejoice in their destruction."

The others objected.

Father turned to Dr. Kling. "You lawyers contribute to this oppression, too. You help the nobility ruin us, and if the preachers are ruined, the ruin of lawyers will follow."

Dr. Kling started to defend himself.

"Don't push us, or you'll pay for it," Father said.

"I'm a lawyer, too," Christopher Blank said, "but an innocent one. It cost me 1500 florins to learn to be a lawyer, and in my practice I get only a few coins for my efforts."

Father was always patient when others talked, but when he talked, people took notes. Sometimes Father himself would say, "Make a note of this," or "Write it down," or "Mark this well."

Hans could see that he enjoyed arguments. Father could quote from memory writers he had read many years ago. For a long time Hans thought everybody had a memory like that, until he himself tried to remember what he had read. There were no two ways about it. Everything that Father was, Hans wasn't. Like everyone else, he hung on Father's words. The only other person who could talk as fast as Father was Mother. Of course, Father always teased her, saying that any woman who talked of anything besides household affairs talked only confusion. Still, he was proud when Mother could quote Bible passages at the supper table right along with the best of the Wittenberg University students studying to be preachers.

Father had no use for certain writers he once honored. Someone mentioned Aristotle.

"Aristotle?" Father snorted. "He thinks that God governs the world the way a sleepy maidservant rocks a child in a cradle."

"Dr. Luther quotes Virgil as fluently as the Bible," a guest remarked in awe.

Every comment like that made Hans cringe. How could he ever catch up with that kind of learning? Still, he could see that the university students asked ridiculous questions at times, and they were far ahead of him in their studies.

One student asked earnestly, "Should you take hold of the communion cup?"

Father smiled. "I always do, so the minister won't miss my mouth. I'm always afraid he won't hit it."

Another asked, "Is baptismal water so consecrated that even if a donkey drank it, it would wipe out sin?"

"No," Father replied. "It's still plain water, even though it's used as a symbol."

Father would sigh at some of the foolish questions. "The philosophers did the right thing when they required their students to remain silent for five years. In Paris no one was awarded a degree in theology who hasn't worked in that field for ten years. In Erfurt only fifty-year-olds were made doctors of theology. Many people were annoyed at my getting my doctor's degree at age twenty-eight." He reflected a moment. "In short, youth is impatient. Take students studying law. Their first year, they are masters of all laws. In their second year, they are experts. By the time they reach the fifth year, they become trembling students. This is the way a boy acts in a bowling alley. First, he expects to strike ten pins, then nine, then six, then three, and at last he's satisfied with one and probably misses the alley at that."

Always interested in what others had to say, Father was sympathetic with Lucas Cranach, the artist, who had a keen interest in Wittenberg affairs.

"Children these days are rebellious," Cranach told Father. "They're not like they used to be. The authorities spend a lot of time with parents and children who can't get along together. There is widespread disobedience and ingratitude. Children aren't like they used to be."

Hans reflected on the artist's remarks. Maybe children weren't really rebellious. Maybe they were just trying to find the right way for themselves.

Father always felt children should know Scripture. After that, they should study and learn other subjects. "House and home may disappear," he would tell students, "but education you can take with you. It will endure."

When he talked about education, Father always mentioned history. He had never studied it in school, and wished he had.

Although Father had begged from door to door as a schoolboy, he did not like the begging that certain monks did for their church. The buildings the monks lived in should be made into good schools for boys and girls, according to him.

As for begging, Father never turned anyone from the door of the Black Cloister, yet he would not accept any money from the publishing of his books to help out the household budget.

Visitors always remarked about printers in a dozen cities printing Martin Luther's books at great profit to themselves.

"Yes," Father said, "they are after me to allow my collected works to be published. I said I'd rather see my books disappear and the Holy Scriptures alone be read. Otherwise, people will rely on such writings and let the Bible go. Who wants to buy such thick books anyhow? And if they're bought, who'll read them? And if they're read, who'll benefit?"

Someone ventured a joke. "Your enemies?"

Father laughed. "I've never had an opponent who fought with me on the same ground. They've always run off on a tangent and haven't stayed on the field of battle. I stand firm. I don't run after anybody. He who pursues somebody gets tired."

Father never gave in. *Neither will I,* Hans thought. Of course, his fight wasn't like Father's. There were no outer enemies, just inner ones. Hans knew he had to fight an inward battle until he found out what he had to do in life.

A NEW LIGHT

FATHER often talked about his enemies. "The pope excommunicated all who spoke up for me. My dear Kathe," he told Mother, "if you went to Rome and admitted that you are Luther's wife, you'd be burned to death." He brooded a moment. "I have bitter enemies."

But Father's eyes sparkled when he mentioned Dr. John Eck of Ingolstadt, his chief opponent through the years. Dr. Eck had been a peasant. He was tall, thick-set, with a loud voice and excellent memory.

"Dr. Eck kept me on my toes," Father said. "He should have been pope. Apart from him, Rome doesn't have anybody." He chuckled. "I remember how he led me into saying that Huss, the Bohemian martyr, had truly Christian ideas that the church could not condemn." Then Duke George, with his enormous gray-white beard falling to his waist, had roared, "Luther is a maniac!"

Father told how Elector Frederick, a huge, ugly man, with small eyes behind rolls of fat, opposed his cousin, Duke George, and protected Father.

Father still fumed at the stubbornness of Duke George. "I'd like to set the old fellow straight. He laughs at me, calls me the son of a bathmaid, and pokes fun at Wittenberg University as a boys' school. It's not decent for a prince to talk like this. I might be the son of a peasant, but I'm also a doctor of the Holy Scriptures."

When someone mentioned the famous scholar Erasmus, who had died the previous July, Father fumed again. "Erasmus was an eel. Nobody could grasp him except Christ alone. He never found out that Scripture is to be followed."

Erasmus had supported Father at first, and then he opposed what Father stood for. Erasmus decided that if there were a God, He would not tolerate what was going on in the world. "He persecuted our cause with ideas which would not occur to a stupid fool," Father raged, "though they are carefully thought out. Here the words from Luke 19:22 apply, 'I will condemn you out of your own mouth, you wicked servant.' "

Father spoke of all his enemies, even Erasmus, as croaking toads. "For ten years I battled with the devil and established all my positions, so I knew they would stand up. But neither Erasmus nor any of the others took the matters seriously. Erasmus stuck to his own affairs — and these were nothing more than heathen business."

Someone mentioned Zwingli, and Father flared again. "I've bitten into many a nut, believing it to be good, only to find it wormy. Zwingli and Erasmus are nothing but wormy nuts."

Of all Father's enemies, Hans thought Andrew Karlstadt the most interesting Father described the seventeen-day disputation between Wittenberg and Leipzig held in the great hall of Pleissenburg Castle, a room hung with tapestries. Dr. Eck's desk was adorned with the picture of St. George and the dragon, and the Wittenberger's desk with Father's patron saint, St. Martin. The choir of Thomaskirche chanted a twelve-part mass. A professor made a two-hour speech on the correct method of disputation. A civil guard in armor paraded every day, with a pipe band.

The Wittenbergers came in two carriages along with two hundred armed students. The Leipzig students carried daggers and swords in their belts. Every day, Dr. Eck went for a ride and came into the hall with riding whip in hand. He poked fun at frail Dr. Karlstadt, who held on to his notes for dear life.

Father's story was enough to keep little Martin and Paul busy for days acting it out. But the most exciting part to Hans, even more than the disputation or the fact that Dr. Karlstadt had presented Father with the doctor's hat and the silver doctor's ring, was that Karlstadt had been persecuted later and came to the Black Cloister and begged to be hidden. For a while not even Mother knew he was there. Father's servant, Wolf Sieberger, took food to Karlstadt every day. Then Father spoke on his behalf and Karlstadt was able to go in safety. He went back to the land, wore the gray smock of peasants, and was called "Neighbor Andrew" by the peasant farmers.

Aunt Lena told the children other exciting details about the disputation at Leipzig. People thought Father's silver ring had magic evil powers, and they were frightened because Father carried a bunch of carnations to his desk and sniffed them from time to time.

"But why were they frightened?" the Luther children chorused. Hans was as curious as the others.

"Because they thought there was some devilish power that your father had hidden on him."

Aunt Lena went on to tell about some of the people who had found refuge at the Black Cloister. Electress Elisabeth of Brandenburg was a Swedish princess and a Lutheran. She was married to a Catholic. Her daughter told on her, and Elisabeth was locked up by her husband. She escaped and came to Saxony. While the Elector of Saxony was getting a castle ready for her, the princess stayed at the Black Cloister. Then her daughter became a Lutheran, and when she found out her mother was sick, she offered to come and nurse her. But there was not room enough. Mother did the nursing.

Life at the Black Cloister seemed quite ordinary now, Hans thought. There were no hidden refugees. People were busy from morning to night. Mother rose at four-thirty every morning to do all her work. She tried to keep the ever-present money worries from Father, who gave everything away as fast as it came in. It was true, as he said, that God provided. "I give myself to the service of the Word and trust the heavenly Father to provide," he said. He told a visitor he had once installed a lathe and learned woodworking in case he had to support his family.

When Mother mentioned a shortage of money, Father would say, "I've taught and preached and written without charging anything. Why should I begin to sell something in my old age?"

Once when Philip Melanchthon mentioned a man who made money by making loans, Mother said, "If my husband had wanted to, he could have become wealthy, too."

Melanchthon disagreed. "That's impossible. Those whose hearts are occupied with public cares can't attend to private ones."

The day-to-day life at the Black Cloister went on. When Mother sometimes had trouble with the servants, Father sympathized in a roar of anger. "They need to be put under the yoke of a Turk. He would measure out to them, day by day, a quantity of work and food, as Pharaoh did to the children of Exodus. Such disobedience provokes God's wrath."

But Mother heard only the word "Turks." "God preserve us from them!" she said, launching into another speech on how the Turks would probably overrun their town.

Father called for courage. "Jonah was sent to rebuke the mighty king of Assyria. That took courage. If we had been there, we would have thought it silly that a single man should attack such an empire. How silly it would seem for one of us to go on such a mission to the Turks. And how ridiculous it has often appeared that a single man should rebuke the pope. But God's work always appears as folly."

Father had the kind of courage he talked about, even though he joked about his lack of humility. "Peter worked as a fisherman and was proud of his skill, though not too proud to take a suggestion from the Master to try fishing on the other side of the boat. I would have said. 'Now, look here, Master. You are a preacher, and I am not undertaking to tell you how to preach.' But Peter was humble, and the Lord therefore made him a fisher of men."

But Father was humble in another way. A group of visiting preachers came to the Black Cloister. One exclaimed, "Doctor, you are so learned you make us all ashamed."

"When I was young, I was learned," Father retorted. "I spoke cleverly. But it was nothing but rubbish."

"But your Bible — " one said.

"Yes, that was my best art, to translate the Scriptures in a way that common people can read and understand them," Father admitted.

"To think that in Saxony there are wives, maidens, students, tailors, shoemakers, bakers, knights, nobles, and princes who know more about the Bible than all the followers of the pope in the world," one of the more talkative preachers exclaimed.

For some reason, Hans disliked the man. He kept smiling and rubbing his hands, eating second helpings at meals, and forever patting little Martin and Paul on their heads.

Hans tried to keep out of his way. He just knew the preacher would ask questions that Hans had been trying not to think about for weeks. But it was no use. The kindly faced, beaming preacher finally cornered him.

"Well, so you are Martin Luther's oldest son."

Hans gritted his teeth. He managed a stiff smile. If only well-meaning people would leave him alone! But no such luck. The visitor was practically purring.

"Are you going to be a famous church doctor, too, and cause a thunderstorm in church?"

Hans shook with a feeling he had never felt before. It wasn't fear, and it wasn't courage. He had to be polite, the way he had been taught. Or did he? What if he blurted out what he really thought and felt?

"No, I — I — " And then it came tumbling out. "I'm my own thunderstorm."

The visiting preacher blinked, looked puzzled, and hurried off.

Why did I say that? Hans asked himself. He had never done such a thing in his whole life, not like that, not to a grown-up.

Suddenly, he felt good, tingling all over, like the first dip into the Elbe River in the spring. He understood why, too.

"You're different," Lenchen said a little later. "What happened?"

"I found out something," Hans said. "I'm not Father."

Lenchen laughed.

"I know that sounds stupid." Hans saw Lenchen frown and hurried on. "I don't mean that. I mean — " He faltered, took a breath, and went on. Lenchen would understand if he could say right out what he discovered. "What I mean is, I don't have

131

to be like Father when I grow up. I only have to be me, myself, the way God intended for me to be."

Lenchen smiled. "I've known that a long time."

She didn't sound superior, just wise.

Hans grinned at her. "Then why didn't you tell me?"

But he had needed to find out for himself, the way boys always do.

Louise A. Vernon was born in Coquille, Oregon. Her grandparents crossed the plains in covered wagons as young children.

She earned her BA degree from Willamette University, Salem, Oregon, and studied music at Cincinnati Conservatory. She took advanced studies in music in Los Angeles, after which she turned to Christian journalism. Following three years of special study in creative writing, she began her successful series of religious-heritage juveniles. She teaches creative writing in the San Jose public school district.

Mrs. Vernon recreates for children the stories of Reformation times and acquaints them with great figures in church history. She has traveled throughout England and Germany researching first-hand the settings for her stories. In each book she places a child on the scene with the historical character and involves him in an exciting plot.

The National Association of Christian Schools, representing more than 8,000 Christian educators, honored *Ink on His Fingers* as one of the two best children's books with a Christian message released in 1972.

Mrs. Vernon is also the author of the following Herald Press juveniles: *The Secret Church* (the Anabaptists), *The Bible Smuggler* (William Tyndale), *Key to the Prison* (George Fox and the Quakers), *Night Preacher* (Menno Simons and the Anabaptists), *The Beggars' Bible* (John Wycliffe), *Ink on His Fingers* (Johann Gutenberg), *Doctor in Rags* (Paracelsus and the Hutterites), *Thunderstorm in Church* (Martin Luther), *A Heart Strangely Warmed* (John Wesley), *The Man Who Laid the Egg* (Erasmus), and *The King's Book* (the King James Version of the Bible).